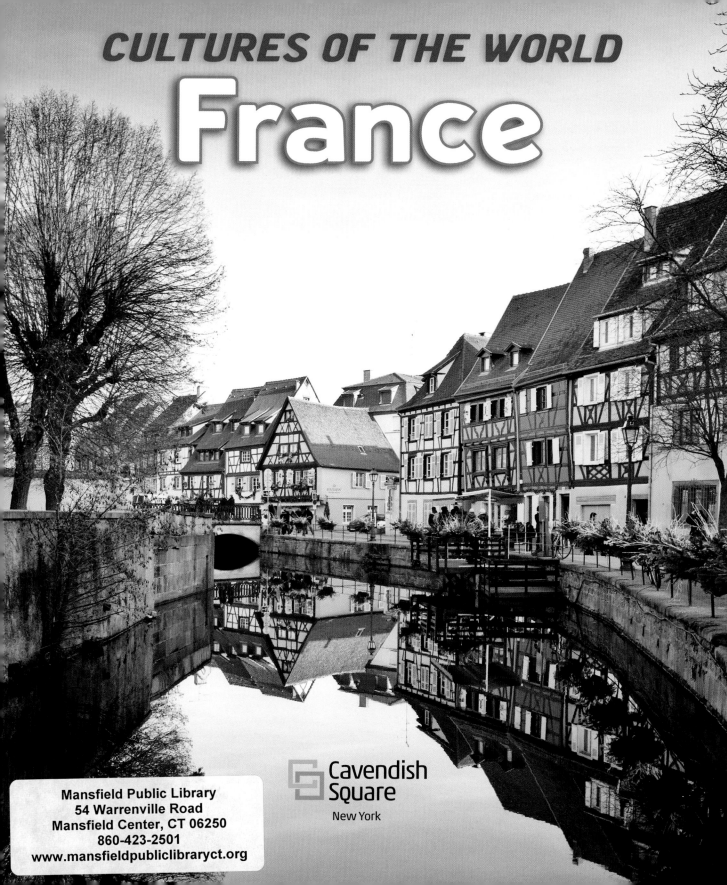

CULTURES OF THE WORLD
France

Cavendish
Square

New York

Published in 2014 by Cavendish Square Publishing, LLC
303 Park Avenue South, Suite 1247, New York, NY 10010

Third Edition

This publication is published with arrangement with Marshall Cavendish International (Asia) Pte Ltd.

Copyright © 2014 Marshall Cavendish International (Asia) Pte Ltd.

Website: cavendishsq.com

Cultures of the World is a registered trademark of Times Publishing Limited.

This publication represents the opinions and views of the author based on his or her personal experience, knowledge, and research. The information in this book serves as a general guide only. The author and publisher have used their best efforts in preparing this book and disclaim liability rising directly or indirectly from the use and application of this book.

CPSIA Compliance Information: Batch #WS13CSQ

All websites were available and accurate when this book was sent to press.

Library of Congress Cataloging-in-Publication Data
Gofen, Ethel, 1937–
    France / Ethel Caro Gofen, Blandine Pengili Reymann, and Michael Spilling. — 3rd ed.
        p. cm. — (Cultures of the world)
    Includes bibliographical references and index.
    Summary: "Provides comprehensive information on the geography, history,
wildlife, governmental structure, economy, cultural diversity, peoples,
religion, and culture of France"—Provided by publisher.
    ISBN 978-1-60870-867-3 (hardcover) ISBN 978-1-62712-158-3 (paperback) ISBN 978-1-60870-873-4 (ebook)
    1. France—Juvenile literature. I. Reymann, Blandine Pengili. II. Spilling, Michael.
III. Title.

    DC33.G54 2013
    944--dc23   2012017630

Writers: Ethel Caro Gofen, Blandine Pengili Reymann, and Michael Spilling
Editors: Deborah Grahame-Smith, Mindy Pang
Copyreader: Tara Tomczyk
Designers: Nancy Sabato, Bernard Go
Cover picture researcher: Tracey Engel
Picture researcher: Joshua Ang

PICTURE CREDITS
Cover: © Steve Vidler / SuperStock
alt.TYPE / REUTERS 34 • AndrewHorne / Wikimedia Commons 100 • Banknotes.com 135 • Corbis / Click
Photos 32 • Getty Images 39, 104 • Inmagine.com 1, 3, 5, 7, 10, 11, 12, 13, 14, 15, 16, 18, 19, 20, 22, 24, 25, 26, 28, 29, 30, 33, 36, 37, 38, 41, 43, 46, 48, 49, 50, 54, 56, 57, 59, 60, 62, 63, 64, 65, 66, 67, 68, 70, 72, 74, 75, 76, 77, 80, 83, 85, 86, 88, 90, 92, 93, 94, 96, 97, 99, 101, 103, 106, 108, 109, 110, 111, 112, 113, 114, 116, 117, 118, 119, 120, 122, 124, 125, 126, 127, 128, 129, 130, 131 • Marshall Cavendish Archives 40, 42, 91

PRECEDING PAGE
The well-preserved old town of Colmar, a commune in Alsace in northeastern France.

Printed in the United States of America

CONTENTS

FRANCE TODAY

MODERN FRANCE IS A COMPLEX MIXTURE OF THE OLD AND new. It is the largest country in the European Union and is the second-largest country in Europe in terms of area. Moreover France is historically central to the development of Western civilization. The name "France" derives from the Latin word *Francia*, which literally means "land of the Franks." The Franks were an early medieval Germanic kingdom that stretched from modern-day southern France to eastern Germany. However, France's cultural makeup includes much more than this Frankish heritage. It is also the home of the ancient Gauls, who resisted the Roman conquest; it encompasses the national identity forged during the Hundred Years' War with neighboring England; it is the land of Louis XVI and the extravagant, aristocratic ancient régime, which was eventually overthrown by the French Revolution of 1789; the land of Napoleon Bonaparte, conqueror of much of Europe; and the center of a colonial empire stretching from North America, via Africa, to Southeast Asia. France's colonial legacy is evident in the ethnic makeup of modern France, with communities from places as far apart as Tunisia, Vietnam, Guadeloupe, Senegal, and Madagascar living in the cities of Paris, Marseille, and Lyon.

France is one of the six founding members of the European Union (EU), and one of the driving forces behind European integration. It is also one of the leading contributing countries to NATO (the North Atlantic Treaty Organization).

This rich history has led to the emergence of a unique cultural blend, where the traditional rural and new, multicultural, urban lifestyles coexist side by side. Globalization has also opened up France to many other cultures around the world. Life in the cities tends to be more cosmopolitan and with a much more diverse mix of ethnic groups than in the countryside. In the cities, people tend to live in apartments, many of them dating back to the 19th century, while in the towns and in the country, most people live in houses with their own yards.

France is bordered by six main countries: Belgium, Luxembourg, and Germany to the northeast; Switzerland and Italy to the southeast, across the Alps; and Spain to the southwest, on the other side of the Pyrenees mountains. In addition, two principalities of Andorra and Monaco border France. The United Kingdom is across the English Channel, which the French call *La Manche* (literally, "the sleeve"). France is often regarded as the natural gateway to Europe.

The sheer physical diversity of the French landscape is one of its great attractions, ranging from the craggy coast of Brittany and the gentle meadows of the Loire Valley to the canyons of the Pyrenees and glacial peaks of the Alps. Each region is very distinct with its own special feel, with food and often a local dialect that is specific to the area. Regional identity remains important to many French people. Small but visible independence movements have sprung up in areas, such as Brittany, the island of Corsica, and the Basque region of the southwest, providing a focus for local nationalism as well as protest against central government policy and control.

The land—and especially agriculture—are central to the French identity, which is obvious from the pride people take in their region and local cuisine. One of the most striking features of the French countryside is the sense of space, especially compared to France's more urbanized neighbors Belgium, Britain, and Germany. In many places, there are huge areas of woodland and undeveloped land without a building in sight. The strength of local and rural identity has also meant that hundreds of towns and villages have evolved very slowly over the years, with many old houses and streets retaining many of their original features.

Ask most people what they know about France, and they will mention good food and wine, spectacular *châteaux* (SHAH-toe), or landmarks known the world over, such as the Eiffel Tower, Sacré Coeur, the Norman abbey of Monte Saint Michel, and the glorious palace of Versailles. They might also mention the jet-set lifestyle of the Cote d'Azur towns of Nice and Saint Tropez; skiing in the Alps; enjoying the wine and hospitality of Bordeaux and Burgundy; the Celtic culture, language, and mythology of Brittany; the famous fizz of the Champagne region; or the farm produce of Normandy, including local cider and camembert cheese. But scratch below the surface and change is afoot.

A UNESCO World Heritage Site, The Château de Villandry castle-palace in Indre-et-Loire features the famous Renaissance gardens, which include ornamental flowers and vegetable patches, all laid out in formal patterns created with low box hedges.

The French economy has undergone major transitions. For much of the last 60 years, the government played a major role in French business, controlling key industries such as power, public transport, communications, and defense. This is because the consensus in France was for the state to control key industries that affect people's quality of life in order to maintain social and material equality for all citizens. In the last decade, however, the center-right government of Nicolas Sarkozy has sought to privatize, or partly privatize, some of these industries, with the government giving up stakes in big companies such as the carmaker Renault, Air France, and France Telecom. There have also been moves to decentralize power and business away from the capital, Paris, and out to the regions in order to solve the chronic unemployment problem.

France remains an extremely popular place for foreigners to visit as well as settle in. More than 77 million tourists took vacations in the country in 2010, making it the world's number-one tourist destination. The French way of life is a hugely attractive pull: Since 1999 France has seen an unprecedented population growth, with the number of residents increasing from 58.5 million in 1999 to more than 66 million in 2013. People from France's former African colonies and Eastern Europe move to France to find work and build a better life for themselves and their families. Other Europeans, especially from countries such as Britain, Portugal, and Spain, move there for an improved quality of life or to retire.

Quality of life is one of the defining characteristics of France today. France regularly scores highly in international quality of life indexes and surveys, and it is not hard to see why. Despite "big government" bureaucracy and high taxes, the country has a first-class health system, some of the best food in the world, and a rich history and culture, and France is a great place to live life. Unlike in some countries, in France it is not considered a shame to pause from the daily rush and just enjoy life. An afternoon break at a local café is seen as an entitlement by many French people. The French are still happy to spend many hours enjoying food, coffee, and good conversation. Pride in their national cuisine and a love of good food is at the core of the French way of life. When time allows, meals are long, sociable family occasions, often taking up several hours in the middle of the day. French meals usually involve three or four courses, including a cheese course before the dessert. Most meals are accompanied by wine and freshly baked bread. Schools in France also allow two hours for lunch, so French children become accustomed to eating multicourse lunches while talking with their friends and family from a young age.

The French also make more time for their personal life. France is among the countries where the working time is the shortest, with more vacations and fewer working hours per week—typically 35 hours. If people work overtime, they will tend to trade it off against more leisure time, rather than seeking to earn more money. It is a similar commitment to leisure time that has led many French people to protest against government cuts in public spending and social provision. Civil agitation and a belief in the right to protest is part of a culture that dates back to the time of the French Revolution.

However, in recent years, the work culture has started to change. In 2008 a law was passed allowing companies to strike deals with unions and individual workers that would allow them to work more than the regulation 35-hour week. Many workers now spend more time in the workplace than in the past and have been less likely to challenge business-friendly working practices since the economic downturn of 2008.

The traditional values of courtesy and smartness are still obvious in modern France. French people, especially the older generation, tend to be polite, bordering on the formal. This national trait is often interpreted as arrogance by foreigners, who fail to understand that the French behave in this way out of respect for themselves and others. Presentation is also considered very important in France, with people taking pride in their clothing—the French won't be seen dressed in a scruffy way. Similarly, stores, homes, and public spaces, such as parks, are all immaculately maintained.

However, this is not to suggest that French culture is uniform throughout the country. On the contrary France is home to a diverse, multicultural society that reflects both the traditions and history of the country as well as its colonial past. Large numbers of people from the former French colonies of the Maghreb countries (Algeria, Tunisia, and Morocco) have moved to France over the last 60 years, and the main urban centers of Paris, Lyon, and Marseille are home to thriving North African communities. The French authorities do not measure people by their ethnic or religious background in national censuses, so it is difficult to give precise figures on the ethnic background of the French population. However, estimates suggest that North African communities make up approximately 6 percent of the total population. In the Île-de-France, as the Paris suburbs are known, they make up as much as 20 percent of all residents. Other immigrants come from sub-Saharan African countries, such as Ivory Coast, Niger, and Cameroon, or southeastern Europe.

About 5 to 10 percent of people in France are Muslim. Islam is the second most practiced religion in France after Roman Catholicism—a consequence of the large number of North Africans who have emigrated to France over the last 60 years. Studies suggest that among Western countries, France is a place where Muslims more easily integrate and feel the most at home. Muslims and non-Muslims all happily coexist side by side; however racial tensions exist, especially in the city suburbs. The wearing of the *hijab* head covering among Muslim girls has also raised controversy in schools. In a commitment to secular principles that separate church and state, French law disallows the wearing of any type of religious clothing in schools. Muslim girls have been expelled from schools for wearing the *hijab*, and this has caused much controversy and some resentment among the Muslim population.

Despite these social challenges and the economic downturn of recent years, France remains a tolerant and diverse country at ease with itself and its place in the world. As the French say, "*plus ça change, plus c'est la même chose* (The more things change, the more they stay the same)."

GEOGRAPHY

The Verdon Gorge, in southeastern France (Alpes-de-Haute-Provence), is one of Europe's most scenic river canyons. About 15.5 miles (25 km) long and up to 0.4 miles (700 m) deep, it has been carved out of limestone cliffs by the turquoise-green Verdon River. Near the French Riviera, it is a popular spot for kayaking, hiking, and rock climbing.

1

F RANCE IS BLESSED WITH FERTILE soil and a pleasant climate. A great diversity of landforms exists: snowcapped mountains, wide plains, dense forests, windblown seacoasts, extinct volcanic cones, ancient underground caves, and sunny Mediterranean beaches.

The country is roughly hexagonal in shape and covers 248,572 square miles (643,801 square kilometers). It is about 600 miles (966 km) long and 600 miles (966 km) at its widest point. Corsica, southeast of the French mainland in the Mediterranean Sea, accounts for 3,351 square miles (8,680 square km) of the total land area.

The Calvi harbor in Corsica, a French island in the Mediterranean Sea.

The natural arches and the pointed cliffs in Étretat, Normandy, have attracted many famous artists, such as Eugène Boudina, Gustave Courbet, and Claude Monet.

France shares land borders with Belgium, Luxembourg, and Germany to the northeast; Switzerland and Italy to the east and southeast; and Spain and Andorra to the southwest.

Most of France's boundaries are natural: the Atlantic Ocean and the Bay of Biscay to the west, the English Channel to the northwest (separating France from England), and the Mediterranean Sea to the southeast. On the mainland, the Pyrenees Mountains lead into Spain, the Alps and the Jura Mountains border Switzerland, and more Alpine peaks act as a barrier between France and Italy. The Rhine River flows between France and Germany. Where no natural barriers exist (such as the border with Luxembourg and Belgium), France has in the past been vulnerable to invasion by foreign armies.

MAIN GEOGRAPHICAL REGIONS

The widely varied landscapes of mainland France can be divided into different geographical regions, each with its own unique beauty.

THE BRITTANY-NORMANDY HILLS lie in northwestern France across the eroded remains of ancient rock. The low, rounded hills and rolling plains of the area are covered with relatively infertile soil. The rugged coastline of Normandy and Brittany is dotted with many bays and is home to both tiny fishing villages and the major seaports of Le Havre and Cherbourg.

Important products from this region include apples, which are used to make cider and an alcoholic drink called Calvados; dairy foods such as Camembert cheese and Normandy butter; and fish from the Atlantic Ocean.

Brittany, with the highest percentage of Roman Catholic churchgoers of any French region, also has a small group of extremist Bretons who want to separate from the rest of the country. An ancient Celtic language is still spoken here, and ancient standing stones recall the ancestors.

THE FRENCH ALPS are part of a great chain that extends across Europe. In France the Alpine peaks, known as the Massif du Mont Blanc, are crowned by the highest peak in the chain at 15,771 feet (4,807 meters)—Mont Blanc. Also in eastern France, the folded limestone Jura Mountains extend into neighboring Switzerland. The waterpower from these mountain streams is harnessed to generate hydroelectric power. The French Alps also boast many ski resorts. The lowest area in France is the Rhône River delta in the far south, which is a mere 7 feet (2 m) above sea level.

The department of Yonne in Burgundy. Burgundy, near the center of France, is a region known for its wine, Roman ruins, beautiful *chateaux*, and quaint Medieval towns.

THE RHÔNE-SAÔNE VALLEY in the Rhône-Alpes region is a major wine-producing area. In the southeast of France, it is an extensive valley separating the Alps from the central plateau of France. The river in the north is called the Saône, becoming the Rhône in the south. Tourists flock to the Rhône Valley to ski in the Alps, visit the historic cities of Provence, and ride horses in the Camargue. This area is dominated by the industrial city of Lyon, second only to Paris in size. Lyon has been famous, for many centuries, for its cooking and for producing silk and synthetic fabrics.

THE NORTHERN PLAINS include the capital city of Paris, the economic, cultural, intellectual, and industrial center of France. Surrounding Paris is the Paris Basin, which includes the historical regions of Beauce (located between the Seine and Loire rivers), Brie, Île-de-France (one of France's most populous areas), Soissonnais, and Valois. Drained by the Seine, the Paris Basin consists

of lowlands made up of sedimentary beds of limestone, sand, and clay. The loamy and fertile soil that has been developed as rich farmland and thick woodland supports a dense population. The Paris Basin, together with southwestern France, is where most of France's grain is produced.

THE FRENCH RIVIERA is an international playground of great beauty. Washed by the Mediterranean, this region contains many altitudes, from mountains and charming hill towns down to coastal plains and sandy beaches. Marseille (France's chief seaport) and the tiny independent country of Monaco are in this area, as are the renowned resort cities of Nice and Cannes. The inland region of Provence-Alpes-Côte d'Azur is characterized by impressive Roman ruins, medieval buildings, ancient olive groves, and even bullfighting arenas. Many famous French artists have tried to capture the luminous daylight of the French Riviera.

THE NORTHEASTERN PLATEAUS include the populous and industrialized provinces of Alsace and Lorraine. These plateaus are crossed by the Ardennes and Vosges mountain ranges. The lower slopes and valleys are dominated by farms and vineyards. Lorraine has iron and coal deposits in addition to Alsace textile and chemical industries. This is also a major milk- and beef-producing area.

THE MASSIF CENTRAL is the largest of France's geographical regions, covering one-sixth of the country. High granite plateaus are cut in many places by deep gorges. Extinct volcanic cones known as *puys* (PWEE), some topped with chapels or religious statues, are a striking feature of the area. At Vichy naturally hot mineral springs have led to the development of health spas. Vichy's mineral water is also bottled for export to distant countries. The soil is poor in most of the Massif Central, and the area is thinly populated. In recent years many people from this part of France have moved to Paris to look for work.

A COUNTRY NOURISHED BY WATER

Throughout French history, rivers have brought fertility to the land and nourished flourishing centers of population. These rivers, with their lesser tributaries and a vast system of linking canals, have enabled the French to cross their country by boat and barge.

France's most important rivers include the Loire (628 miles or 1,010 km), the Seine (478 miles or 770 km), the Garonne (404 miles or 650 km), the Rhône (324 miles or 522 km), the Saône (298 miles or 480 km), the Rhine (118 miles or 190 km), the Somme (150 miles or 241 km), and the Marne (325 miles or 523 km). The Loire is the longest river running entirely within France. Glorious chateaux, or castles, sit on its banks (below). The slow-moving Seine connects Paris with the Atlantic Ocean. The wine-producing seaport of Bordeaux lies on the Garonne estuary, its location making it an ideal home for merchants and shipbuilders.

Lyon lies at the point where the Rhône and Saône rivers meet, and its heart is a peninsula between the two rivers. Since the Rhône-Saône Valley receives relatively little rainfall, the Rhône, originating from Lake Geneva in Switzerland, provides both hydroelectric power and irrigation to farms and vineyards in the region. Hydroelectric power for Alsace and Lorraine is supplied by the Rhine, which flows along the French-German border.

A complex system of canals aids the movement of goods between smaller cities and towns. Picturesque examples are the Nantes-Brest Canal in Brittany and Pays de la Loire, the Canal du Nivernais in Burgundy, and the Canal du Midi, running from Toulouse in the Midi-Pyrénées region to the Languedoc-Roussillon coast.

The valley of Champagny le Haut, in the Côte-d'Or department of Burgundy, is one of the gateways to the Vanoise National Park.

THE PYRENEES MOUNTAINS separate France and Spain in a sparsely populated region of the southwest. Many of the sheer mountain peaks top 10,000 feet (3,048 m). Farmers raise cattle and sheep on the slopes and foothills. The Midi-Pyrénées (the largest region in France in terms of surface area) town of Lourdes, with its reputation for miraculous cures, attracts millions of Roman Catholic pilgrims every year.

THE AQUITAINE BASIN is a lowland region known for its fruit orchards, the Bordeaux wine industry, oil and natural gas fields, steel mills, and chemical factories. Extensive forests, rolling plains, huge sand dunes, and beaches are characteristic features of this area.

TERRITORIES

France is divided into 22 administrative regions: Alsace, Aquitaine, Auvergne, Brittany, Burgundy, Centre, Champagne-Ardenne, Corsica, Franche-Comté, Île-de-France, Languedoc-Roussillon, Limousin, Lorraine, Lower Normandy, Midi-Pyrénées, Nord-Pas-de-Calais, Pays de la Loire, Picardy, Poitou-Charentes, Provence-Alpes-Côte d'Azur, Rhône-Alpes, and Upper Normandy. These regions are subdivided into 96 *départements* (day-par-tun-MAHN), or departments.

From its colonial past, France has jurisdiction over many overseas departments and territories: French Guiana in South America, Guadeloupe and Martinique in the Caribbean, Réunion and Mayotte in the Indian Ocean, and Saint-Pierre and Miquelon in the North Atlantic Ocean. Areas also dependent on France include Corsica, French Polynesia, and New Caledonia.

CORSICA—L'ÎLE DE BEAUTÉ (THE ISLE OF BEAUTY)

The island of Corsica lies in the Mediterranean Sea about 105 miles (169 km) from the southern French coast and 56 miles (90 km) from Italy. The island has a population of around 356,000. Over the centuries, Corsica has been conquered by invaders from Greece, Rome, Pisa, and Genoa. In 1768 Genoa sold its rights over Corsica to France, and the island became a département *of France following an invasion by French troops in 1769.*

Corsica's coast is marked by steep, rocky cliffs leading to rugged mountains. Poor soil and heavy forests limit the amount of land given to agricultural use. Some inhabitants fish and raise sheep, and others cultivate crops or work in industries based on hydroelectric development. Tobacco growing supports about one-quarter of the economy. Tourism is the primary source of the island's income. Its sandy beaches, palm trees, and dramatic scenery draw visitors from around the world. Many villages have remained virtually unchanged for hundreds of years. Corsica is covered by lush vegetation, notably the macchia underbrush. The island's plants produce a fragrance that even carries out to sea, giving the island the nickname "The Scented Isle."

Napoleon Bonaparte, who became emperor of France, was born in the capital city of Ajaccio on August 15, 1769.

In Corsica traditional loyalties to family and clan have led to lengthy, sometimes deadly, vendettas. In fact, the word vendetta, *meaning a hereditary blood feud, came into the English language from Corsica. For example it is estimated that between 1821 and 1852, no fewer than 4,300 murders were committed in Corsica.*

More recently Corsican zeal has inspired a guerrilla battle for greater autonomy from France and for cultural recognition. The Corsican language, a form of Italian, is widely spoken in the home, although the French government has banned its use in schools. Corsican nationalists, particularly those from the Front de Libération Nationale de la Corse (Corsican National Liberation Front), have not hesitated to use terrorist tactics to further their separatist aims.

In 1991 Corsica was granted the status of territorial collectivity (collectivité territoriale). *In 1999 the controversial Matignon Process was started, involving representatives of the French government and leaders of Corsica, to grant Corsica greater legislative autonomy. However, in a referendum held in 2003, a narrow majority of Corsican voters rejected the plan to grant greater autonomy by combining the two* départements *of the island into a single region with greater powers. Since that time separatists have again resorted to violence, and there was a spate of minor bomb attacks around the time of the French presidential elections in April and May 2007.*

CLIMATE

Despite its geographic diversity, France's climate is generally moderate, due to the effects of the North Atlantic Drift from the west and the Mediterranean Sea in the south—all of which are favorable to cultivation. There are three broad climatic zones: the oceanic northwest, with warm summers and chilly winters; the Mediterranean southeast, with hot dry summers and mild winters; and the continental northeast, with cold winters and light rain throughout much of the year.

Western France receives winds from over the Atlantic Ocean that bring rain, cool winters, and moderate summers. The Gulf Stream in the Atlantic Ocean tempers the climate and makes it more moderate than at comparable latitudes in North America. Light misty rain is common throughout most of the year.

Inland there is a more pronounced seasonal difference, with hotter summers, colder winters, and clearly defined wet and dry periods.

Eastern France and the mountainous areas experience severe winters and stormy summers. The Vosges Mountains contribute to Alsace's sharp, cold winters and warm-to-hot summers. Alpine peaks above 9,000 feet

The lush green landscape of the Vosges Mountains in Alsace.

THE CAMARGUE

The Camargue is a triangular river delta where the Rhône meets the sea—a marshy island bounded by two branches of the Rhône and the Mediterranean Sea. The Camargue is Western Europe's largest river delta, with exceptional biological diversity, and home to unique breeds of Camargue horses and Camargue bulls, and to more than 400 species of birds, including pink flamingos. Camargue horses are a small, hardy breed used to round up Camargue bulls (below). The Camargue horse is one of the oldest breeds in the world, and is closely related to the prehistoric horses whose remains have been found elsewhere in southern France. Measuring just 13 or 14 hands (a horse's height is measured in units known as hands, which equal 4 inches, so 13 to 14 hands would be 52 to 56 inches) in height, Camargue horses are more the size of ponies and are much smaller than the typical modern horse.

Covering more than 360 square miles (932 square km), the area is a vast plain dominated by dozens of brine lagoons, or étangs, which are cut off from the sea by sandbars and surrounded by reed-covered marshes. Roughly a third of the Camargue consists of either lakes or marshland, and the region is a haven for numerous marsh-dwelling birds and animals. Most of the area received regional park status in 1970 as part of the Parc naturel régional de Camargue (Regional Nature Park of the Camargue).

There are few towns in the Camargue. With a population of around 55,000, the area's capital is Arles, located at the extreme north of the delta, where the River Rhône forks into the Greater Rhône and Lesser Rhône. The only other towns of note are Saintes-Maries-de-la-Mer, about 32 miles (51.49 km) to the southwest, and the small Medieval fortress-town of Aigues-Mortes on the far western edge.

There is a profusion of flowers in France. Some are used in the perfume industry while others, like rapeseeds, are used to produce oil.

(2,743 m) and Pyrenean peaks above 10,000 feet (3,048 m) are snowcapped all year-round. The French Riviera has a dry, warm climate. Occasionally cold northerly winds known as the *mistral* blow through southeastern France at a brutal 65 miles (105 km) per hour—enough force to damage crops.

FLORA AND FAUNA

More than a quarter of France is covered with trees and plants. These vary with the climate from one part of the country to another. In the northern and central regions, forests of oak, chestnut, pine, and beech trees are common. In the low-lying marshes, willows, poplar, and cypress trees may be found.

On the western border, carefully planted pine forests thrive where swamps have been drained. Brittany's landscape, largely a bleak expanse of moors with scrubby brush and stunted trees, contrasts greatly with the Provençal landscape of ancient olive trees and verdant grapevines and fruit trees. In other parts of France, cypress, Spanish chestnut, and ash trees form thick groves and forests. Evergreens such as cushion pine, dwarf pine, and juniper flourish in parts of the Alps.

Wheat, barley, corn, and oats are among the chief crops in France. The total grain harvest was 62 million tons (57 million metric tons) in 2010. The area devoted to grains is 33 million acres (13 million hectares), including 22 million acres (9.5 million ha) for cereals. Lavender, thyme, and other herbs, buried truffles, and mushrooms in rich variety scent the fields and flavor the tables of France.

The Atlantic and Mediterranean coasts offer a colorful palette of shellfish and other sea creatures. Oysters and lobsters caught off the coasts of Normandy and Brittany, and trout and salmon caught off the southern coasts delight diners throughout the country.

Flamingos, herons, and storks ripple the lake waters of nature reserves in the province of Lorraine. Wild animals include the brown bear, wild boar, polecat, wildcat, and deer. Majestic white horses and black bulls roam the nature reserves of the marshy Camargue region in the Rhône River delta. Smaller mammals commonly seen in the French countryside include badgers, bats, beavers, foxes, hares, hedgehogs, moles, rabbits, squirrels, and weasels. Farmers depend on cattle, chickens, hogs, and sheep for a living. The rare chamois and marmot can be spotted in the Alps and the lynx in the Pyrenees Mountains.

INTERNET LINKS

http://kids.nationalgeographic.com/kids/places/find/france/

This website provides facts, videos, maps, history, travel videos, flags, maps of countries and cities of the world from *National Geographic*, and photographs of France aimed at a junior audience.

http://news.bbc.co.uk/2/hi/europe/country_profiles/3028038.stm

A brief summary of the geography, culture, and politics of Corsica, with facts, maps, photographs, and links to recent news stories are provided in this website.

www.midi-france.info/07020201_camargue.htm

This is a website that offers facts, photographs, maps, and other information about the landscape and culture of the Camargue region.

www.terragalleria.com/photos/?keyword=france-landscape

With a particular emphasis on mountain regions, Terragalleria shows 75 spectacular photographs of landscapes throughout France by the professional photographer QT Luong.

www.franceinphotos.com/

This commercial photographic library offers hundreds of photographs of the French landscape, including rivers, towns, and historical features.

HISTORY

The Pont du Gard is a giant bridge aqueduct built by the Romans in about 19 B.C. to carry water to the city of Nîmes over the Gard River. Three tiers of arches rise to a height of 155 feet (47 m). The first tier is composed of six arches, the largest spanning the river; the second tier is composed of 11 arches of the same dimensions; the third, carrying the conduit, is composed of 35 smaller arches.

TWO THEMES DOMINATE French history. One is the drive to forge a unified nation out of diverse peoples; the other is the quest for glory. France wanted, and still wants, to embody the most cultured and enlightened civilization in the world.

EARLY SETTLERS

Prehistoric cave dwellers are estimated to have inhabited France as far back as 750,000 years ago. Celts were the first tribes known to have invaded the region some 2,000 to 4,000 years ago. The Celtic legacy lives on today in Celtic words in the French language and in megalithic monuments in Brittany.

The Romans named the Celtic territories Gaul. These territories included modern-day France, northern Italy, the southern Netherlands, and Belgium. The Gauls were a warrior society and fought fiercely against the Roman invasion in 58 B.C. However, the Roman emperor Julius Caesar defeated the Gallic chief Vercingetorix at the Battle of Alesia in 52 B.C., and the Romans ruled Gaul for the next 500 years. They left behind road systems, towns, cities, a legal system, taxes, and winemaking.

In the fifth century A.D., the Germanic Visigoths, Burgundians, and Franks pushed into the area that is now called France. The Visigoths settled in the Provence and Aquitaine regions in the south, the Burgundians occupied much of the Rhône Valley, and the Franks settled in the northeast. The Frankish king Clovis I defeated the last Roman

ruler in 486 and later established the capital of the Merovingian dynasty in Paris. By the seventh century the Merovingian dynasty had been displaced by the Frankish Carolingian dynasty. The greatest Carolingian ruler was Charlemagne (742—814), who ruled much of Western Europe from 771 to 814. Conquering territories in Spain, Germany, and northern Italy, he was crowned Holy Roman emperor in 800. After his death, his empire was divided among his three grandsons into areas roughly equivalent to modern-day Germany; Belgium, the Netherlands, France's Alsace and Lorraine regions, and northern Italy; and France (mainly Aquitaine in the southwest and the region around Paris).

BUILDING THE STATE: THE MIDDLE AGES

After the Carolingian dynasty, during the feudal period of the Middle Ages, the Capetians ruled France from 987 to 1328 with perseverance and a practical sense for politics. They were descendants of Robert the Strong (820—866), count of Anjou and Blois. Robert's great-grandson, Hugh Capet (939—996), the first Capetian king, was succeeded by a further 13 kings. They laid the foundation for the French nation-state, but feudalism weakened their power.

Charlemagne, or Charles the Great, was king of the Franks from 768 and emperor of the Romans from 800 to 814.

Noble lords received royal land in exchange for service to the king, and many became more powerful than the king did. By the 11th century France was a mosaic of feudal domains, each with its own separate power base. The most powerful was that of William II (later called William the Conqueror), duke of Normandy, who invaded England in 1066 and became king of England.

During the Crusades from the 11th to the 13th centuries, the Capetian kings strengthened their power across France. Philip II Augustus (1165—1223) was one of the most important kings of this period. Together with King Richard the Lionheart of England, he led the Third Crusade (1189—1192) to the Holy Land, although the two kings later fought over their various land possessions in France. Philip defeated an alliance of his enemies at the Battle

Saint Joan of Arc, also called the Maid of Orléans, was born in 1412 to a farming family in the northern village of Domrémy in Lorraine. At age 13, Joan claimed to have heard voices from God directing her to be a good girl. When she was 17, the voices told her to leave home and save France and the king.

Joan was determined to obey these voices. She sought an audience with the dauphin, the eldest son of the late king Charles VI. The dauphin had been disinherited by the English in the Treaty of Troyes in 1420. Joan convinced the uncrowned king and his advisors that the siege of Orléans would be the battle to end the Hundred Years' War. Dressed in armor, Joan led French troops to victory at Orléans on May 8, 1429. She then led French troops and the dauphin through English-occupied territory to Reims for his coronation as King Charles VII.

During the siege of Paris in 1430, Joan was captured by the Duke of Burgundy and delivered to the English. Holding fast to her faith and denying that the voices she had heard were demonic, she was tried by an English-dominated Church court and condemned as a witch. At the age of just 19, she was burned at the stake in Rouen on May 30, 1431.

It is said that the spirit of the Maid of Orléans enabled the French army, who then believed that God was on their side, to finally drive the English out of France. Joan had also revived France's devotion to the monarchy. Almost 500 years after her death, in 1920, Joan of Arc was canonized by Pope Benedict XV to become Saint Joan of Arc.

of Bouvines in 1214, and he was able to successfully annex Normandy and Anjou from the English Crown. By the 1330s France was the most powerful kingdom in Western Europe. During the Capetian reign, intellectual life made great progress. Universities were founded, and the University of Paris became the center of philosophical and theological studies in the Christian world. Much of the success of the Capetian kings was due to 300 years of unbroken succession from father to son.

Louis XIV (1638—1715) was the personification of the quest for glory and the embodiment of absolute power. King of France from 1643 to 1715, he saw himself as God's representative on Earth. France was the leading European power during King Louis's reign. Louis extended France's eastern borders with three major wars: the Franco-Dutch War, the War of the League of Augsburg, and the War of the Spanish Succession. He also brought the nobility, the justice system, and the military under his control. Much of his success, however, could be attributed to his brilliant counselor, Jean-Baptiste Colbert.

Louis built a magnificent palace at Versailles, still one of the architectural glories of Europe. He attracted the most gifted artists, architects, writers, engineers, and scientists to his court. However, his disregard for the common French people, his decadence, and his persecution of the French Protestants, which caused many of them to flee France, set the scene for the eventual downfall of the French monarchy.

A political struggle for power, in particular over the legitimate succession to the French Crown, led France and England to war in 1337. Periodic battles, known collectively as the Hundred Years' War (1337—1453), continued for the next 116 years. The English kings, especially the Plantagenet dynasty, claimed sovereignty of territory throughout western France, dating back to the time of the Norman conquest of England. The war was interrupted by a monstrous plague, the Black Death, which killed up to half of all the people in Europe. When fighting resumed, the English nearly conquered all of France. However, the religious zeal, patriotism, purity, and courage of the young Joan of Arc helped turn the tide of the war.

Lasting from 1756 to 1763, the Seven Years' War was a gargantuan struggle for power, involving most of the major European states. It stemmed from rivalry between Great Britain and its ally Prussia with France and Spain for colonies and trade in India, West Africa, and especially North and Central America. The war was characterized by sieges and arson of towns as well as open battles involving extremely heavy losses; it is estimated that between 900,000 and 1.4 million people died during the war. With Prussia fighting French forces in Europe, Britain was able to concentrate on gaining control of North America and establishing domination of the seas with its powerful navy. French forces were eventually expelled from India, North America, and much of the Caribbean, severely limiting France's colonial ambitions, as the British Empire grew. France did gain some revenge, however, by helping the American colonists in gaining independence from Britain during the American Revolutionary War (1775—83).

THE REFORMATION

By 1500 the boundaries of present-day France were established under the Valois kings. It was also during their reign that the ideals of the Renaissance spread to France from Italy.

A religious movement called the Reformation in the second half of the 16th century gave rise to a new school of Western Christianity called Protestantism. The work of German reformer Martin Luther (1483—1546) first appeared in France in 1519, and anti-Catholic placards began to appear in Paris and other French towns by the 1530s. This led to civil war and Catholic persecution of the French Protestants, called Huguenots. In the terrible days that followed, 3,000 Huguenots were massacred at once in Paris on Saint Bartholomew's Day in 1572, and perhaps another 8,000 in other provincial cities.

The wars ended when Huguenot leader Henri of Navarre converted to Roman Catholicism and was crowned King Henri IV in 1594, the first of the Bourbon kings. Henri signed the Edict of Nantes in 1598, granting the Huguenots religious and civil liberties. The next two kings, Louis XIII and Louis XIV, known as the Sun King, were absolute monarchs, holding great power.

THE FRENCH REVOLUTION

The seeds of the French Revolution were planted in part by philosophers of the Enlightenment spreading new ideals of government and justice and in part by the anger of the rapidly growing but generally impoverished population over the injustices that existed in society.

In 1789 King Louis XVI tried to deal with the crisis by assembling the States General, consisting of three classes: clergy, nobles, and commoners. However, the clergy and nobles clashed with the newer class of commoners, who broke away and declared themselves the legal National Assembly, formed not of the old elites but "of the people." The king mustered 20,000 royal troops to Paris. Believing that he was planning to suppress the new assembly, an angry mob stormed the Bastille prison on July 14. Peasants revolted in the countryside and fighting erupted in the cities. The National Assembly seized control. Traditional privileges were removed from the nobles and clergy, and the feudal system ended. In 1791 a new constitution changed the absolute monarchy into a constitutional monarchy. The National Assembly divided the old regions of France into 83 *départements* of roughly similar size. All *départements* were run by elected councils. The old taxes were abolished and replaced by new ones.

King Louis and Queen Marie Antoinette tried to flee the country but were arrested and forced to sign the new constitution. Royalists and counterrevolutionaries opposed the assembly, and in April 1792 France went to war against pro-monarchist Austria and Prussia. Fear of counterrevolutionaries in the Parisian prisons led to the mass execution of more than a thousand prisoners. The king and queen were killed.

The French Revolution then entered a second, more radical phase. Extremist Jacobins under Georges-Jacques Danton, Jean-Paul Marat, and Maximilien Robespierre rose to power and set up the Commune of Paris. Robespierre led the Committee of Public Safety, which inaugurated the Terror—a wave of massacres and executions of enemies of the Revolution.

Some famous personalities of the French Revolution include (clockwise, from left to right) **Abbé Sieyes, Maximilien Robespierre, Honoré Mirabeau, Jean-Paul Marat, and Georges-Jacques Danton.**

"The king must die so that the country can live."
— Revolutionary leader Maximilien Robespierre.

NAPOLEON BONAPARTE (1769—1821)

During the French Revolution a young officer named Napoleon Bonaparte, born in Corsica, rapidly rose to power. Napoleon was an expert artillery officer who quickly rose through the ranks during the early years of the revolution. He had risen to the rank of general by the age of 24, and became a key figure in the revolutionary army following successful campaigns in Italy. In 1799 Napoleon led a successful coup against the government. He quickly installed a new form of government, the Consulate, with himself as first consul.

Napoleon gave France an enlightened civil code (the Napoleonic Code of 1804), religious tolerance, and elite schools, or grandes écoles. He created an efficient central government with a stable currency, reasonable taxes, and founded the Bank of France. He named himself emperor in 1804 and, with his wife Josephine, left a lasting impact on French style and fashion.

A great military strategist and heroic leader, Napoleon conquered most of Europe, winning great victories over various European coalitions, including Austria, Russia, and Prussia. However, his troops were finally stopped in Russia in 1812 by harsh winter weather and a shortage of food. After his defeat in Russia and losing the decisive Battle of Leipzig in 1813, he abdicated in 1814 and was exiled on the island of Elba. A brief return to power, between March and June 1815, ended with Napoleon's military defeat at Waterloo by British and Prussian forces. Napoleon was banished to the island of Saint Helena in the Atlantic, where he died in 1821.

Tens of thousands of people were guillotined in the name of "*Liberté, Égalité, Fraternité*" (Liberty, Equality, and Brotherhood). In 1792 the National Convention abolished the monarchy and proclaimed the First French Republic. France exported revolution abroad to form "sister republics" in Western Europe. Switzerland, northern Italy, and the Netherlands soon came under French influence. An anti-France alliance, consisting of Austria, Prussia, Great Britain, the Netherlands, Sardinia, and Spain, was formed. A temporary

"Better not to have been born than to live without glory."

—attributed to Napoleon Bonaparte.

government, the Directory, controlled France from 1795 to 1799. Many elections, revolts, and purges followed. Napoleon Bonaparte emerged from this chaos to lead France against its enemies and expand its borders. Napoleon successfully defeated Prussia, Russia, and Austria at the Battle of Austerlitz in 1805, but was later defeated following an unsuccessful and debilitating campaign in Russia in 1812—13.

THE SEARCH FOR STABLE GOVERNMENT

Napoleon III and his troops surrendering to Wilhelm I, king of Prussia, after the Battle of Sedan of the Franco-Prussian War.

After Napoleon's defeat, Austrian, Prussian, Russian, French, and British delegates reorganized Europe during the Congress of Vienna (1814—15) and restored France's borders to what they had been in 1792. In the years that followed, France underwent several political changes: it was first governed by a constitutional monarchy, then by an authoritarian empire, and finally it became a republic.

First the monarchy was restored with two more kings of the Bourbon royal family. Their rule was replaced in 1848 by the Second Republic, with Frenchmen demanding a republic and the right to vote. The last king, Louis-Philippe, abdicated in 1848. Thus the rule of the Second Republic was short-lived. Napoleon Bonaparte's nephew, Louis-Napoleon Bonaparte, established the Second Empire and was proclaimed Emperor Napoleon III in 1852.

During the Second Empire, industrial production doubled; foreign trade tripled; the first investment banks opened; and French engineers built bridges, railways, docks, and sewage systems at home and abroad. Louis-Napoleon also liberalized the political system. His reign ended with the French defeat in the Franco-Prussian War (1870—71). The postwar treaty forced France to give the regions of Alsace and Lorraine to the newly formed German empire under Chancellor Otto von Bismarck. The people ousted Louis-Napoleon, and a new constitution became the basis for the Third Republic.

From 1899 to 1905 a coalition of left-wing and center parties provided France with political stability and fostered economic growth. France established a powerful colonial empire in Africa and Asia, rivaled only by Britain. The years between 1890 and 1914 are remembered as *La Belle Époque* (the Beautiful Era). This period witnessed developments in education, the flowering of Paris as a social and art capital, the rise of labor unions, and the separation of church and state. It was a time of beautiful clothes and the peak of luxury living.

TWO WORLD WARS

The massive loss of life in World War I (1914—18), the worldwide economic depression of the 1930s, and defeat by Germany in World War II (1939—45) marked one of the lowest periods in French history.

In 1907 France entered into a diplomatic agreement, the Triple Entente, with Britain and Russia. This was part of European power politics of the time and was intended to limit the power and influence of an increasingly strong Germany. However, following the Balkan crisis (1903—14), troops from all the major European powers were mobilized. Germany invaded France in August 1914, capturing much of Belgium and parts of northern and northeast France during their initial push for ground. Much of the war was fought in northern France, and battle sites such as Flanders, Verdun, and the Somme have become infamous for the deaths of the many millions killed. Soldiers suffered the horrors of trench warfare and new technologies of death: fast-firing machine guns, heavy artillery, and poison gas. Roughly 1.3 million French people perished during the war, and a further million were disabled by wounds.

The United States joined the war on the Allied side (France, Great Britain, and Russia) in 1917. Following the defeat of Germany in November 1918, Alsace and Lorraine were restored to France, but the French economy had suffered greatly. Economic growth was set back a decade, and production fell to 60 percent of prewar levels. Recovery was dependent on German reparations. To rebuild manpower, immigration restrictions were relaxed and about 2 million foreign workers entered France.

GENERAL CHARLES DE GAULLE (1890—1970)

One of the monumental figures in 20th-century France was General Charles de Gaulle. During World War II, in exile in England and sentenced in absentia to death by a pro-German French Vichy court, he courageously opposed the Nazis and formed the Free French Forces, sending radio broadcasts to his French compatriots from London. His heroic resistance movement spread throughout France and helped overpower Nazi occupation.

De Gaulle headed two provisional governments after the war, but he resigned in 1946. He opposed the Fourth French Republic and its constitution, which he did not think improved on the Third Republic's inadequacies. In 1947 de Gaulle formed the Rassemblement du Peuple Français *(Rally of the French People), which obtained 120 seats in the National Assembly but was later disbanded.*

In 1958 de Gaulle had an opportunity to return to power when the insurrection in Algiers brought France to the brink of civil war. De Gaulle was elected to a seven-year term as president on December 21, 1958. He developed a new constitution, establishing the Fifth Republic. Under this constitution the president's powers were greatly increased, while those of the parliament were reduced.

De Gaulle worked hard to make France a strong, independent power, free from the domination of either the United States or the Soviet Union during the Cold War. He saw France as the rightful leader of Europe. De Gaulle urged France to join the European Economic Community (EEC), also called the Common Market, in 1957. He recognized the People's Republic of China, helped create an independent French nuclear-weapons program, and removed all French forces from NATO command in 1966.

De Gaulle was a tall, striking man, who seemed in his very person to symbolize French glory. The French people admired his courage and integrity. Yet many eventually began to resent his arrogance, which made him seem at times more a king than a president. De Gaulle's leadership survived student uprisings and widespread strikes that paralyzed the country's economy. He finally resigned in 1969 after the French rejected his constitutional reforms. He quietly retired to his country home, where he died the following year.

In the 1930s the world entered into an economic depression, known as the Great Depression. This led to political turmoil. In France right-wing movements grew in strength. In Germany Nazi leader Adolf Hitler ascended to the chancellorship, supported by millions of jobless and dissatisfied Germans.

In September 1939 Germany invaded Poland, dragging France and Britain into World War II. In May 1940 Germany invaded France. Unprepared France fell quickly, and Germany occupied the northern two-thirds of France, including Paris. A pro-German government was established in southern France, called Vichy, under Marshal Philippe Pétain, a World War I hero. In 1942 southern France was also occupied. During this time some French collaborated with the Germans for their own advancement. Others formed an underground resistance. On June 6, 1944, Allied soldiers landed in Normandy and with the aid of local resistance forces liberated France over the course of the next two months.

General Charles de Gaulle at the consultative assembly of 1945.

With the defeat of Germany and the end of the occupation, a new constitution written by the National Assembly in 1945 created the Fourth Republic, which was led by General Charles de Gaulle. That year French women voted for the first time. France rebuilt itself with much help from the U.S. Marshall Plan, where the United States lent money to European countries to help build their economies following the devastation of the war. In 1949 France became a charter member of the North Atlantic Treaty Organization (NATO). The Allied victory over Germany ultimately restored France's prewar boundaries.

POSTWAR FRANCE

After World War II Paris regained its intellectual and cultural vibrancy. Both world wars had shown the importance of political choices for individuals. Existentialist philosophers such as Jean-Paul Sartre (1905—80) and Albert Camus (1913—60) depicted mankind alone in a godless universe, where man finds self and meaning of life through free will, choice, and personal responsibility.

France's outgoing President Nicolas Sarkozy (*left*) welcomes newly elected president François Hollande (*right*) at the Élysée Palace before the 2012 handover ceremony in Paris.

France lost control of important colonies during World War II. Indochina was taken by the Japanese during the war; after the war France regained control only of southern Indochina after communist forces had seized the north. After eight years of bloody struggle, France withdrew, and the former colony was divided into Cambodia, Laos, and North and South Vietnam.

France faced similar calls for independence among its North African colonies in Tunisia, Algeria, and Morocco. In 1954 rebellion broke out in Algeria, and a long and brutal struggle ensued. Fear that the rebellion would spread to Morocco and Tunisia led the French government to make drastic concessions to these two countries, granting them independence in 1956. The costly war in Algeria lasted past the 1950s, sharply dividing the French and inspiring terrorist violence. In 1962 Algeria finally gained independence.

The president who succeeded Charles de Gaulle was Georges Pompidou, who served from 1969 until his death in 1974. He made significant contributions to the development of France's nuclear proficiency and a new defense plan. Valéry Giscard d'Estaing, leader of the Independent Republican Party, took over with a coalition government and served as president from 1974 to 1981. With the election of President François Mitterrand of the Socialist Party (*Parti Socialiste* or PS) in 1981, government ownership of services and resources increased. Mitterrand was elected for a second term in 1988. Socialists also controlled Parliament until 1986, when Jacques Chirac, the conservative mayor of Paris, became prime minister. (This was the first case of "cohabitation," with a prime minister from a different coalition than the president.)

MODERN FRANCE

In 1990—91, French troops were involved in the war against Iraq as part of the broad coalition to eject Saddam Hussein's forces from Kuwait. In 1992 France ratified the Maastricht Treaty establishing the EU. In the election of 1993, conservative Édouard Balladur became prime minister under François Mitterrand. In 1995 Jacques Chirac was elected president for seven years, and in 1997 socialist Lionel Jospin was appointed prime minister for the next five years. In the mid-1990s French troops and agencies were also involved in peacekeeping operations in the Balkans, and French forces joined the 1999 NATO bombing of the Federal Republic of Yugoslavia in response to Yugoslav aggression in neighboring Kosovo.

In 1999 the euro was introduced to replace the French franc, creating a shared currency for 17 countries of the 27-member EU. In 2002 Jacques Chirac was reelected to the presidency for five years by a resounding 82 percent against right-wing nationalist Jean-Marie Le Pen.

Nicolas Sarkozy was president of France from 2007 to 2012, when he lost to Socialist François Hollande. Following the financial crises that started in 2008 and the recent economic downturn, French politics has been dominated by domestic concerns over the viability of the euro, the banking crisis, and government debt. High unemployment remains a very big problem in France, especially among young people.

INTERNET LINKS

http://greatmilitarybattles.com/Battle%20of%20Alesia.htm

This website provides illustrations, maps, and photographs of the Battle of Alesia that took place between Caesar's Roman army and Vercingetorix's Gauls in 52 B.C.

www.luminarium.org/encyclopedia/100years.htm

This website from Luminarium offers a detailed account with illustrations and links to all of the main figures in the Hundred Years' War.

www.louis-xiv.de/index.php?

This comprehensive website offers a detailed biography of the life and times of the Sun King, Louis XIV, with portraits and links to accounts of the court, castles, people, and ideas of the period.

www.napoleonguide.com/index.htm

This website provides detailed information and links on the life of Napoleon Bonaparte, including articles, quotes, maps, and photographs.

GOVERNMENT

The country town hall may be housed in a charming building with great historical character, such as this one in Calais.

3

FRENCH THINKERS AND LEADERS have aspired over the centuries toward different ideals of good government. At many points in French history, kings, courtiers, peasants, and soldiers of every class have engaged in bloody battles for the power to rule.

Over the course of its history, France has witnessed many different forms of government, including feudalism, absolute monarchy, constitutional monarchy, empire, and now parliamentary democracy.

NATIONAL GOVERNMENT

France is a democratic republic, with its capital in Paris. Since 1958 the government has been known as the Fifth Republic. The president of this

The offices of the Conseil d'Etat, the supreme body consulted by the French government before a new law is passed.

Flags of the European countries fly outside the Council of Europe in the city of Strasbourg, Alsace. The Council of Europe is an international organization promoting cooperation among all countries of Europe in the areas of legal standards, human rights, democratic development, the rule of law, and cultural cooperation.

parliamentary democracy is elected by all voters (citizens age 18 or older) for a five-year term. (Up until 2002, the term of office was seven years.) The president appoints the prime minister, who then recommends to the president the other ministers who form the Council of Ministers, the French cabinet. The prime minister oversees the government's day-to-day affairs, while the president, as head of state, focuses on the direction of national policy and foreign affairs.

As part of a system of checks and balances, France's national government has separated power into three branches: (1) The executive branch is headed by the president and the prime minister. (2) The legislative branch is the parliament, which is made up of two houses: the National Assembly and the Senate. (3) The judicial branch consists of a system of courts.

Until September 2004 the Senate had 321 senators, each elected to a nine-year term. In 2004 the term was reduced to six years, while the number of senators was increased to 348 in 2011, in order to reflect changes in the makeup of the country's population. The members of the Senate are indirectly elected by department electoral colleges. In 2011 the Socialist Party won control of the French Senate for the first time since the foundation of the French Fifth Republic.

The National Assembly has 577 deputies elected by majority vote from the same number of single-member constituencies for five-year terms. The National Assembly is the more powerful of the two houses.

THE PRESIDENT

In France the president is an elected head of state. The president holds the nation's most senior office, and outranks all other politicians. With an official residence in the Élysée Palace in Paris, the French presidency is the oldest presidency in Europe. General Charles de Gaulle greatly increased the power of the president. Although it is the prime minister and parliament that make many of the nation's laws, the French president wields significant influence. As head of state the president can dissolve the National Assembly and call for new elections at any time. The president also appoints the prime minister. In an emergency the president can assume almost complete power. In 2012 François Hollande, candidate for the French Communist Party, was elected president for a five-year term with 51.6 percent of the votes.

The Élysée Palace in Paris is the residence of the president. It holds his office, and is where the Council of Ministers meets.

LOCAL GOVERNMENT

France is divided into 22 decentralized *régions* (RAY-giohn) for planning, budgetary policy, and national development. An earlier system, still in use, divided France into 96 *départements*. Each *département* has a main town and is run by a general council responsible for welfare, health, administration, and departmental employment services. It also has a prefect representing the national government, and a local president.

The *départements* are divided into smaller units called *arrondissements*. These are in turn subdivided into cantons and communes. There are about 36,500 communes in France, ranging in size from small villages to entire cities. The communes are run by mayors elected by local municipal councils. One of the mayor's duties is to perform marriages. In France there is a "political class" of men and women whose entire working lives are spent as professionals in government service.

A famous image of French punishment has long been the guillotine. Originally used in Europe for executing criminals of noble birth, it was adopted during the French Revolution as a more humane, egalitarian, and quick way to execute a criminal, as compared with hanging, beheading, or quartering. The man whose name it bears, Dr. Joseph-Ignace Guillotin (1738—1814), was a physician and a member of the National Assembly. He influenced the passing of a law requiring all death sentences to be carried out using this decapitation machine, which he is said to have described as "a cool breath on the back of the neck." The guillotine has also been called "the national razor" and "the widow." The guillotine was seldom used in the 20th century and last used in 1977. The death penalty was abolished in France in 1981.

POLITICAL PARTIES

It is thought that describing political parties as left-wing or right-wing stems from the French Revolution. During that time the radical reformers, the Jacobins, sat on the left side of the National Assembly, and the conservatives sat on the right.

In France today, parties on the left include the Socialist Party of France (*Parti Socialiste de France*) or PS, the smaller French Communist Party (PCF), and the Left Radical Party (PRG). On the right are the New Center (NC), Movement for France (MPF), and the largest right-wing party, the *Union pour un Mouvement Populaire* (UMP). Outside, the main political groupings are the conservative and xenophobic National Front (FN) and the Democratic Movement (MoDem), the latter a centrist liberal party established in 2007 by

the presidential candidate Francois Bayrou. In the 2007 National Assembly elections, the right-wing parties led by President Nicolas Sarkozy won 345 seats, whereas the left-wing parties gained 227 seats.

The leftist parties support public ownership or control of most industries but, in practice, have cooperated with private business since the 1930s. Both the socialists and communists support strong, government-financed social security and medical benefits. The rightist parties want less government regulation of the economy.

CRIME AND PUNISHMENT

French law cases are decided entirely on the basis of written law. French law is based on the constitution of the Fifth Republic, itself inspired by the Napoleonic Code. This means that besides the regular court system, there is a separate court system to deal specifically with legal problems of the French administration and its relation to the French citizen. A constitutional council rules on constitutional questions.

French *départements* have both civil and criminal courts, with Courts of Appeal for each. Cases involving murder and other serious offenses are heard in the Courts of Assizes. For serious criminal cases, a court is made up of a three-judge panel and a jury of nine jurors who together make verdicts and, if a conviction is handed down, also decide the sentence. The highest court of the land is the Court of Cassation. Unlike the U.S. Supreme Court, it does not make a final decision. It can criticize legal proceedings and refer a case back to the lower courts to be reconsidered. In France judges are appointed for life.

The French tend to be lenient about crimes of passion. When it is deemed that a normal person was driven by extreme emotion to commit murder, the penalty is less harsh.

"Every French presidency takes on some of the flavor of a royal court....The French adore the political leader who shows a mystic identification with the nation's rural roots....The political leader has to communicate a deep sense of history, to intone the great themes of the French nation."— Richard Bernstein, American journalist, columnist, and author.

The French Flag

The French flag is called the tricolor because it is divided into three equal vertical stripes of blue, white, and red. These colors were first used as a French emblem during the French Revolution. On July 17, 1789, King Louis XVI wore a tricolor knot of ribbons on his hat, combining the colors of Paris—red and blue—with white, the color of the royal family. France has no official coat of arms.

The Legion of Honor and Other Decorations

The highest French honor for outstanding military and civil service is the Légion d'Honneur *(Lay-JYOHN DON-er), or Legion of Honor (below), created by Napoleon Bonaparte in 1802. During World War I the* Croix de Guerre *(KRWAH duh GEHR), or Cross of War, commended bravery in battle, while the* Médaille Militaire *(May-DIE meelee-TAIR), or Military Medal, was awarded to both combatants and noncombatants during World War I.*

THE ARMED FORCES

The president of France heads its armed forces. About 2.3 percent of the country's gross domestic product (GDP) is spent on defense. Major reform of the armed forces was initiated in 1996 to professionalize the armed forces and eliminate the compulsory 10-month military service young Frenchmen had to serve. This was replaced in 2001 by a one-day session for all 17-year-old boys and girls to educate them on careers in the military. In 2008 President Sarkozy ordered a review of French defense policy, and radical changes have been made so that French forces are more adapted to meeting global threats.

In 2011, 251,000 professional soldiers served in the army, navy, and air force. A further 105,000 volunteers between the ages of 18 and 30 also serve in the gendarmes as militarized state police under the Minister of Defense, distinct from the National Police Force under the Minister of the Interior.

France has nuclear arms and is a major supplier of weapons to several countries, including Singapore, United Arab Emirates, India, and Pakistan. General Charles de Gaulle once said, "There is no corner of the earth where, at any given time, men do not look to us and ask what France has to say." This country's military and foreign policies do continue to affect the rest of the world. In recent years French troops have deployed in anti-terrorist operations in Afghanistan and Mali, and have carried out peacekeeping missions in the Balkans, Ivory Coast, Haiti, Lebanon, and Libya.

Numbering approximately 7,600 troops, the French Foreign Legion, staffed mainly by foreign volunteers, is part of a tradition of foreign troops who have served France since the Middle Ages. Formerly focused on French interests in Africa, the French Foreign Legion has increasingly become a peacekeeping force.

French police-men patrolling the streets of Toulouse. A distinctive feature of the French police is the *képi* (keh-PEE), the cap worn by police officers.

INTERNET LINKS

http://flagspot.net/flags/fr.html#ori

This website is dedicated to the French tricolor, including its construction, use, and role in French public life.

www.nndb.com/honors/139/000048992/

This website provides a comprehensive account of the list of Legion of Honor winners, both past and present.

www.legion-recrute.com/en/

This website describes the life of a member of the French Foreign Legion, with pictures and firsthand accounts of the recruitment process.

ECONOMY

The plowed fields in Auvergne, a predominantly agricultural region in France. While agriculture is important, Auvergne is also well known for its tire industry, represented by Michelin.

4

F RANCE IS ONE OF the world's
most highly developed economies.
Modernization of French industry
began in the early 1950s, and national policy
has encouraged a tremendous growth in
production and trade since World War II.

The economy
of France is
highly developed
and complex,
with industry,
manufacturing,
banking, tech-
nology, tourism,
and agriculture
all contributing
to the wealth
of the country.

Huge factories equipped with computers and machinery have replaced the typically small, pre-war manufacturing enterprise. Many workers have left farms to staff the country's growing industrial centers.

France is among the world's top producers and consumers of nuclear power and offshore oil technology. It was the world's fifth-largest industrial economy in 2012, when France's GDP was US$2.25 trillion. France is in the middle of a euro zone crisis. Severe austerity measures are being implemented through cuts in government spending and tax credits in an attempt to control the budget deficit by 2013. Unemployment was 10.3 percent in 2012, as compared with 7.4 percent in 2008. The French government intervenes directly in the economy. Although this is slowly changing, the government still owns or partly owns many important industries to protect them from foreign competition.

FERTILE SOIL

Of all France's natural resources, its soil is the most vital. A huge portion of French land is fertile, supporting crops such as wheat and sugar beets, fruit orchards, vineyards that generate the fabled wines of France, and grassland for grazing livestock. Agriculture, including fishing and forestry, used to be the backbone of the French economy but now accounts for only 1.9 percent of the GDP.

The Arc de Triomphe, in the center of Place Charles de Gaulle in Champs-Élysées, is one of the most famous monuments in Paris. France is one of the most popular tourist destinations in Europe, with tourism helping to boost the economy.

Acres of forests cover much of the French countryside. The timber is used for construction and making furniture and paper. Although forests are being destroyed at an alarming rate almost everywhere in the world, French forests are actually expanding as a result of careful government planning and reforestation.

The French have used their land resources wisely. The application of modern farming techniques, combined with government subsidies for farmers, has helped make France a leading agricultural producer. Chief products include wheat, fruit (such as apricots, apples, grapes, and peaches), cattle, milk, potatoes, pigs, and chickens. France grows most of its own food and also exports wheat and dairy products, mainly to other members of the EU.

MINERALS

France has significant deposits of iron ore and bauxite (aluminum ore). The land also yields coal, gypsum, natural gas, petroleum, potash, salt, sulfur, tungsten, and zinc. France is a major producer of uranium, which is used for nuclear energy and weapons. French ores are used to produce aluminum and steel, essential materials for France's growing industries.

THE SERVICE INDUSTRIES

Seventy-nine percent of the GDP comes from the service industries. In the past half century there has been a notable shift in employment away from agriculture and manufacturing into services. Seven out of every 10 French workers is now employed in industries such as education, health care, trade, banking, tourism, insurance, transportation, and communications. About 79.5 million tourists visited France in 2012, making it the most visited country in the world.

In recent years tourism has become one of France's great growth industries. In 2010 about 77 million tourists visited the country, and the number was almost as high in 2011, with 76 million visitors. These numbers made France one of the most visited countries in the world in 2011, with the country gaining the third-largest income in the world from tourism. Tourism accounts for 6 percent of GDP, although two-thirds of this is as a result of internal tourism.

The attractions for both the foreign visitor and French people vacationing in their own country are obvious. Whether you prefer skiing in the Alps, enjoying Parisian culture and nightlife, sunbathing on the Mediterranean coast, or enjoying the rich, wine-producing valleys of Bordeaux and Burgundy, there is something for everyone. And the standard and variety of cuisine is uniformly high across the country. The capital, Paris, is the most visited city in the world. Paris is a magnet for tourists, with world-famous attractions such as the Eiffel Tower, Arc de Triomphe, the cathedral of Notre-Dame, the Louvre museum, the palace at Versailles, and so on bringing in many millions of visitors every year.

Three-quarters of tourists are Europeans, with the British, Germans, and Dutch the most frequent visitors.

DESIGN AND MANUFACTURING

France is one of the most developed countries in the world, and industry accounts for 18 percent of France's GDP, with roughly one out of every four workers employed in industry. The diversified industrial sector includes electronics, food processing, metallurgy, mining, and the production of aircraft, automobiles, chemicals, machinery, steel, and textiles.

Products that the rest of the world associates with France are often luxury items, such as perfumes, gourmet foods and wines, and dyes and fine fabrics for the fashion industry. France also exports various high-tech products, such as the world's fastest trains, sophisticated electronic equipment, military airplanes and rockets, and communications satellites. Helicopter manufacturing and shipbuilding also continue to be important industries.

FRENCH LUXURIES: PERFUME AND FASHION

The production of perfume has long been a major industry in France. French perfumes are exported to more than 100 countries. Since the 1920s famous fashion designers—Chanel, Yves Saint Laurent, Christian Dior, Patou, and many others—have lent their names to perfumes and reaped fortunes.

Flowers grown in the south of the country, especially around the town of Grasse, have been used to make fragrances since the 16th century. Fields of lavender, carnations, lilies of the valley, and other flowers brighten the countryside around Grasse.

Today plant oils, animal extracts, and less costly synthetic ingredients and chemicals are also prime ingredients in perfumes' closely guarded formulas. These formulas are tested by expert sniffers, mostly men, who are referred to in the business as "noses."

The French fashion industry is also famous for its elegance, style, quality, and luxury. Other nations have looked to France for inspirational clothing designs since the 14th century.

In the mid-19th century an Englishman named Charles Worth founded the first couture house in Paris. Thus began the modern tradition of marketing fashion to wealthy women from many countries using beautiful models in seasonal fashion shows. New designs are quickly copied in less expensive versions.

French and foreign designers based in Paris influence the look of everything from ball gowns to sportswear, men's clothing, shoes, jewelry, and other accessories throughout the world. Fans of French fashion claim that a silk scarf with the Hermès (right) label can turn any outfit into the epitome of chic.

The automobile industry illustrates French talent for technical innovation and daring design. French engineers invented the clutch, gearbox, and transmission shaft and introduced the front-wheel drive system. Renault and PSA Peugeot Citroën are both among the top ten largest car manufacturers in the world.

The French talent for design has also contributed to the manufacture of aircraft, such as the Caravelle commercial jet plane, the supersonic airliner Concorde, and the Mystère and Mirage jet fighter plane. Arianespace, the world's leading launcher of commercial satellites, has its main offices located in Paris.

The world-famous aircraft maker Airbus is also based in France. The A300 series has been an important commercial carrier since the late 1960s. In recent years Airbus has introduced its A380-800 wide-body aircraft, capable of carrying up to 850 passengers. With a range of 9,600 miles (15,400 km), the A380 can fly nonstop from New York to Hong Kong, and is a direct competitor with American aircraft maker Boeing's latest long-haul carrier, the 747-8.

Quality and design are exemplified by Michelin tires, Chanel clothing and accessories, Limoges china, and hundreds of other products for which France is famous around the world.

Although Paris is the center of manufacturing, important factories are located throughout the country, and major centers have developed around the ports and coalfields of northwest France. The metallurgical and textile industries have grown rapidly. More recently the government has given cash and other incentives to promote new small factories in outlying regions.

A unique aspect of modern France is the survival of a strong, locally based artisan tradition where products are made by hand or on small-scale machinery. Particular products—gloves, glassware, lace, copper cookware, or knives, for example—are manufactured in towns or villages throughout the country. These industries rely on locally available raw materials or skills passed down the generations.

The C42 Citroën showroom in Champs-Élysées, Paris, was designed by the French architect, Manuelle Gautrand. The automobile industry is thriving in France, with French-made cars exported to many countries overseas.

ENERGY SOURCES

France's energy supplies are derived mainly from imported oil, coal, and natural gas, and domestic hydro-electricity and nuclear power.

Coalfields were exploited for hundreds of years until it became cheaper to import coal from abroad. Because of the shortage of coal reserves, hydroelectric power has been harnessed where possible, such as at rivers and waterfalls in the Alps, Jura Mountains, Pyrenees Mountains, and the Massif Central.

France is one of the world's top producers of nuclear energy for electricity. Nuclear power plants supply about 75 percent of France's electricity.

The management of nuclear power plants in France stresses safety and economy, and thus nuclear power enjoys more popular support than in countries where serious nuclear accidents have occurred.

People's daily lives are affected by the government policy of energy conservation. The aim is to lessen French dependence on outside sources of power. Energy-saving plans include reduced speed limits for drivers (81mph) and limits on home heating levels.

At the mouth of the Rance River on the coast of Brittany, a unique power plant converts the energy of the tides into electricity. Research on alternative power sources, such as solar power, continues.

A nuclear power station in Centrale nucléaire de Cruas in Rhône-Alpes. The many nuclear plants are a direct result of the 1973 oil crisis and the "Messmer Plan," a program that aimed to generate all of France's electricity from nuclear energy.

France is one of the six founding members of the EEC. An important accomplishment of the EEC was the establishment of common price levels for agricultural products.

FOREIGN TRADE AND THE EUROPEAN UNION

France is the world's fifth-largest exporter of goods (mainly durables such as machinery and transportation equipment) and ranks second in services and agriculture. It is the leading producer and exporter of farm products in Europe. Its major imports are petroleum products, machinery, agricultural goods, chemicals, vehicles, aircraft, plastics, and iron and steel products. Major exports are machinery, automobiles, aircraft (such as the highly successful Airbus series), plastics, pharmaceuticals, chemicals, agricultural products, iron and steel products, electronic and telecommunications equipment, textiles and clothing, and wines and brandies.

DEBT CRISIS IN THE EURO ZONE

The European currency, the euro, officially came into existence in 1999, bringing monetary union to the majority of countries in the EU. Only the United Kingdom, Sweden, and Denmark did not join. Following the financial crisis and credit crunch that started in 2008, many European governments struggled to borrow money to pay their rising costs and debts. In December 2009 Greece, one of the smallest members of the EU, admitted it had debts of 300 billion euros (US$400 billion)—the highest national debt in modern history. Much of this debt had accumulated because of high government spending—spending that was greater than the money they received in taxes. Before the crisis, the Greek government had been able to borrow from various European banks to service their debt, but after the financial meltdown of 2008, they struggled to raise more cash. Concerns also developed over other heavily indebted countries, such as Portugal and Ireland. Along with Greece, these countries only account for 6 percent of the EU's total GDP—but the seriousness of the debt crisis affected the entire EU.

In 2010 and 2011 the EU created a number of emergency loans and the indebted countries were forced to introduce tough limits on public spending that caused riots in some cities, especially the Greek capital, Athens. Large banks in France and Germany were heavily exposed to the debts of these countries as well as their own debts, and this in turn affected the financial stability of the euro zone as a whole. Banks in France are estimated to hold $56 billion in Greek loans. In early 2012, as part of a new loan package agreed to by the European Central Bank (ECB), the International Monetary Fund (IMF), and the EU, Greece agreed to introduce an austerity budget to cut their huge budget deficit. These measures have significantly reduced living standards in Greece, throwing many Greek families into poverty.

The massive amounts of money owed by Greece and other indebted countries have cast doubt on the future of the euro and European monetary union. The continuation of the debt crisis has also made it difficult for all member countries of the EU to grow their economies.

France was a founding member of the EEC in 1958. Charles de Gaulle had envisioned the EEC as a world power bloc, inspired by France to remain independent of the United States and the Soviet Union. The EEC is now called the EU. Currently France trades primarily with Germany, Spain, the United Kingdom, Italy, and the United States.

France participated in the 1992 Treaty of Maastricht, a project aiming to create a single economic area for Europe, to be on a more even economic footing with the United States. Member countries opened their frontiers and removed customs barriers and import taxes. The currencies of 12 countries were absorbed into the single currency, the euro, in January 2002, bringing monetary union to 300 million people across Europe. The success of the EU has always depended on the cooperation among all its members. France, however, is also concerned to maintain its national autonomy and prestige.

TELECOMMUNICATIONS AND TRANSPORTATION

The French had an electronic communication system called Minitel that predated the Internet. More than 10 million telephone subscribers have a computer terminal in their home at no extra charge. They can use it to find numbers, make airplane and train reservations, order theater tickets, shop for goods and services, and "talk" via electronic mail. However, in the last decade, most French people have become connected to the Internet, both at home and at work. French high schools are equipped with one computer for every six students. Cellular phones are also widely used.

Although the postal system is still owned and run by the French government, telephony and telecommunications have been privatized, with heavy competition between companies such as France Telecom, Cégétel, and AT&T for fixed lines; Bouygues Télécom, SFR, Orange SA, and Itinéris for cellular phones; and AOL, Wanadoo, Club Internet, and Tiscali for Internet connections.

In 1981 the *Train à Grande Vitesse* (Tran ah Grahnd Vee-tehss), or TGV, meaning "High-Speed Train," began running between Paris and Lyon in the Rhône Valley. It now covers many destinations from Marseille and Perpignan in the south to Brussels in the north and Bordeaux in the southwest to Strasbourg in the east. The world speed record set by the TGV in 1990 was 320.3 miles (515.3 km) per hour, making it the fastest passenger train in the world. However, the average speed on daily runs is closer to 162 miles (261 km) per hour. The TGV Eurostar was first opened in 1994. It connects the French capital, Paris, with the British capital, London, via the Eurotunnel. Since upgrading the line in 2003 and introducing a faster train, High Speed 1, in 2007, the train can cover the distance in a record time of 2 hours, 15 minutes.

French commercial airlines include Air France, Air Inter, AOM, and Air Liberté. France's 5,280 miles (8,500 km) of waterways transport heavy cargo, such as agricultural products, fuel, and raw materials. Paris is the most important river port in France, followed by Strasbourg.

INTERNET LINKS

www.parisfashionshows.net/

This website includes an extensive sample of photographs from the Paris Fashion Show from 1997 to 2011.

www.world-nuclear.org/info/inf40.html

This website from the World Nuclear Association includes detailed information on France's nuclear power stations.

http://ambafrance-us.org/spip.php?article949

This website compares energy sources, especially nuclear power, of France and the United States.

www.airbus.com/galleries/

This famous French aircraft manufacturer's website includes photos and videos showing Airbuses from every angle and explaining how an Airbus is built.

www.peugeot.com/en/200-years-of-history/200-years.aspx

This website includes a history of one of France's biggest car and cycle makers, Peugeot, with video and photo galleries.

www.terroir-france.com/

This is a colorful guide to perhaps France's most famous export, wine. It covers the main wine-making regions of France, with maps and photographs and links to sections on wine-making and grape varieties.

ENVIRONMENT

A lavender field in Provence adds a gorgeous shade of purple across the landscape.

E COLOGICAL AND environmental protection is a government priority and a major public concern in France. The Ministry for the Protection of Nature and the Environment (Ministère de l'Ecologie, du Développement Durable, des Transports et du Logement—MEDDTL [formerly MEEDDAT]) was formed in 1971 with a mission to monitor the quality of the environment, protect nature, and prevent or reduce pollution.

Starting in 1975 many laws were passed, and many public and semipublic environmental agencies set up.

NATIONAL PARKS

France has a rich flora of some 4,500 plants and is home to some 93 mammal, 269 bird, 32 amphibian, 32 reptile, and 53 freshwater fish species. Sadly a number of animal species, including the gray wolf, have become extinct and 28 are endangered, including the ibex, slender-billed curlew, Mediterranean monk seal, Corsican red deer, river otters, and numerous species of bats.

France started creating protected areas in the 1960s. About 7 percent of France is designated as a protected conservation area. There are 10 national parks in France, 45 regional nature

The brick-built Pont d'Espagne bridge that spans the Gave de Marcadau at the point where it meets the Gave de Gaube, high in the Pyrenees National Park.

parks, 156 nature reserves, and 429 protected coastal sites. These provide a haven for specific species of animals, birds, and fish. Human settlement and industry are forbidden in these areas. Regional nature conservation boards manage these protected areas in partnership with local authorities and private partners, buying or renting land to protect irreplaceable habitat areas.

The Pyrenees, with its breathtaking landscapes, lilies, chamois, griffon vultures, and astonishing midwife toads, is the most popular park. The Vanoise, Mercantour, and Ecrins national parks are located in the Alps, and the Cévennes National Park is south of the Massif Central. The Guadeloupe National Park extends over two islands: Grande-Terre and Basse-Terre. Port-Cros covers both land and sea: the islands of Port-Cros, Bagaud, Gabinière, and Rascas, and a 0.4-mile (600-m) marine belt around them. The newest national parks are the Guiana Amazonian Park, the Reunion National Park, and the Calanques National Park.

BLACK TIDES AND COASTAL PROTECTION

France has a powerful strategy to protect its coasts. Coastal land is purchased by the government to protect it from urbanization, careless tourist projects, and industrial and domestic pollution. Authorities have had to act on a large scale several times in recent French history to clean hundreds of miles of beaches in Brittany from oil spilled from tankers.

The first devastating oil spill came from the *Torrey Canyon* in 1967, followed by the infamous *Amoco Cadiz* in 1978, and more recently the *Erika* in 1999. The *Erika* collapsed next to Belle-Île, an island off the southern coast of Brittany, and soiled 275 miles (440 km) of coastline. The *Amoco Cadiz* disaster, which spread 220,000 tons (220 million kg) of oil across 225 miles (360 km) of coastline around Portsall in the north of Brittany, killed or hurt 30,000 birds and destroyed one-fourth of all the region's oysters.

Sadly many cargo ships still routinely pollute the shores by illegally cleaning their tanks in the open sea. Environmental teams and volunteers try to clean up the beach and animals affected by the spilled oil.

GROWING FORESTS

France has some of the largest forests in Europe: they cover some 28 percent of its territory. Observing that the Alpine, Pyrenean, and Massif Central environments were fragile and degraded, French officials in 1860 initiated an unprecedented policy of mountain reforestation. Today France maintains this careful plan of reforestation to compensate for the industrial and agricultural use of wood, growing forests by around one percent annually. The program's major enemies are forest fires and fungus. Every summer the south of France and Corsica are ravaged by forest fires, destroying more than 173 square miles (448 square km) of forest annually.

Damaged trees from a forest fire in France.

Acid rain has given French forests a reddish tinge even in the greenest of springs. For most trees, there is no cure and they die slowly, and are not replaced by new growth. At the end of 1999 severe storms destroyed forests and killed people in Europe, wiping out in a couple of nights what the French forestry industry would have consumed in nine months and disfiguring the landscape, including the historical gardens in the palace of Versailles.

POLLUTION

France has joined in most of the international agreements concerning industrial hazards and general pollution, including the Seveso rulings. These agreements cover the main polluters: quicksilver, lead, and cadmium, present in most industrial waste.

Asbestos, an insulation material widely used in buildings, has been found to cause cancer. The discovery that entire universities and schools were polluted with a cancer-causing substance raised a scandal. A wide-ranging

CONSERVATION

The nature parks have been an important part of a tricky and ambitious conservation plan—to reintroduce next-to-extinct species in areas where they have almost disappeared.

Brown bears have been imported to populate the Pyrenees. In collaboration with neighboring Italy and Switzerland, France has brought lynx and hawks from Central Europe, raised them in captivity, and carefully released them into the wild in the Alps. After years of effort and overcoming many unexpected difficulties, the organizers have brought a bear population of next to zero to a fragile but promising community of a dozen or more, saving them from extinction in France.

The same initiative has been introduced for wolves in different areas, including Ardèche, with much less popularity among the farmers and neighbors, who are afraid for their cattle or for themselves.

The storks winter in tropical Africa and India and during spring migrate back to Europe to nest and reproduce. It is common in Alsace to see huge nests on top of the chimneys of houses, whose owners are proud and considered lucky. Yet an extensive plan has been implemented to prepare suitable solid poles to welcome nests and to cover high-tension electrical power lines, where hundreds of young storks get killed every year.

One can also see bridges unconnected to roads and tiny tunnels in Picardy. They adorn highways in the middle of nowhere for the sole benefit of boars, deer, and hogs that would get run over and crushed by cars if they crossed directly on the highway!

program was implemented to remove the material and to protect students and workers from asbestos dust.

France has also subscribed to the Kyoto Protocol (1997), agreeing to limit greenhouse gas emissions. An air quality law was passed in 1996, but France fell short of the intended objectives, mainly because of the uncontrolled rise in car usage. To fight this problem, the government is trying to promote public transportation across France. One initiative is car-free days, created in 1998 and involving 66 cities by 1999. People are urged to leave their cars at home on car-free days and use public transportation or bicycles. A study by the French Agency for Environmental Health Safety published in 2011 showed that about 5,000 people are killed by urban pollution—that is, pollution caused by cars, trucks, and buses—annually.

KEEPING THE WATER CLEAN

France's water reserves are abundant but unequally distributed. Six regional agencies control the use and safety of water supplies. Some mineral water companies, such as Evian, Vichy, and Perrier, are under scrutiny. France introduced the "who pollutes, pays" rule to finance the protection and cleaning of its used water. The main dangers to clean water come from the abusive use of chemical fertilizers, the illegal dumping of industrial waste, and the growing needs of the population. In 2007 high levels of nitrate pollution were found in the drinking water in Brittany. Since then France has been trying to implement measures to improve water pollution.

FOOD SAFETY

Toxic algae washed up on a beach in Brittany.

Food security is no longer an issue in Europe, but food safety has become a major concern. Mad cow disease is one striking example. The scare first started in Britain in 1996. Measures have been taken in France to slaughter all sick animals and forbid the sale and import of contaminated meat, from the United Kingdom in particular.

A strict and comprehensive monitoring structure has been put in place to control cultivation, preparation, and storage to ensure that French food is wholesome. More and more farmers have switched to organic farming, and bio-labels have been created to ensure that products called "bio" are free of chemical fertilizers.

Ecologists in France have a widespread mistrust of genetically modified plants. They contend that the cultivation of these plants upsets the ecological balance and that eating them may prove dangerous. They want strong regulation and scientific monitoring to ensure that all risks are understood and analyzed. There are three bodies that hold responsibility for monitoring public health and regulating products intended for human consumption—

GLOBAL WARMING

Together with other countries in the EU, France is working toward reducing its carbon emissions by 20 percent by 2020 in accordance with the Kyoto Protocol of 1997. France, however, has more ambitious aims and plans to reduce its emissions by 75 percent by 2050. France has implemented many initiatives, including improving energy efficiency in buildings, promoting the use of more environmentally friendly vehicles, banning the use of incandescent light bulbs and replacing single-paned windows with double-paned ones. With all these changes in place, France hopes to take the lead in the fight against global warming.

A wind turbine in the French countryside. France still lags behind other European nations in its investment in wind power.

the French Food Safety Agency, the French Health Products Safety Agency, and the French National Health Watch Institute.

WASTE DISPOSAL

Each year French households produce more than 24 million tons (24 trillion kg) of waste, more than double the amount 30 years ago. In 2004 each person produced 881 pounds (400 kg) of waste. Happily, from 2002 to 2004, household waste actually decreased by 13 pounds (6 kg) per person.

Streamlining French waste management through waste recovery and making waste financially self-supporting is foremost in the minds of French authorities, and they have had some success. Some 55 percent of glass and 45 percent of paper used is recycled. Each city has a specific plan for selective waste disposal: for glass, paper, plastic, and dangerous items such as batteries, printer cartridges that contain lead, car fuel, and car batteries. Waste collection, treatment, and disposal is a growing business in France.

NUCLEAR ENERGY

France made the strategic choice to develop nuclear power in the 1970s, and almost 80 percent of the country's total production of electricity comes from nuclear power. France is the second in the world, after the United States, in nuclear development. As an active nuclear power, France conducted experimental nuclear tests in French Polynesia in 1995 that raised worldwide protests.

Nuclear power does not pollute the air or aggravate the greenhouse effect, but uranium is one of the trickiest substances to handle and must be safely stored for thousands of years. In 1986 fears became reality when the Chernobyl nuclear plant in the Soviet Union burned, sending a huge radioactive cloud into the air. When the cloud drifted over France, government authorities advised against eating fresh produce for a while. With time, the danger seems to have subsided. The Chernobyl incident and the Fukushima nuclear disaster in Japan have raised many doubts about the use of nuclear energy, and France is now exploring alternative nonpolluting energies, such as solar and wind power and energy recycling.

The ecologists have a specific political party, called *Les Verts*, or the Greens, which aims to play a bigger role in major issues such as water safety, industrial waste control, education, and raising awareness about environmental issues among the general population. In 2010 the party merged with Europe Ecologie and together they are now known as L'Ecologie-Les Verts, and the group grew to 13,000 members in 2013.

INTERNET LINKS

www.kwintessential.co.uk/articles/france/Endangered-Wildlife-in-France/539

This website provides information about endangered wildlife in France and what is being done to ensure the survival of endangered and threatened species.

www.planetepassion.eu

This website provides information about various types of wildlife in France, and includes a forum where questions and observations can be presented and discussed.

France reprocesses its own spent nuclear fuel. Belgium, Germany, the Netherlands, Switzerland, and Japan send, or have sent in the past, spent nuclear fuel to France for reprocessing. High-level reprocessed waste is vitrified (solidified) and stored at La Hague for several decades, where it awaits final geologic disposal.

THE FRENCH

A French family in front of a house. The French love children, and the family still forms a strong unit in the community.

6

A LTHOUGH AROUND 63 million people live in France, the country is so large that it has a relatively low population density (about 295 people per square mile, or 114 per square km) when compared with other countries in Europe. In addition the overseas departments and territories are home to about 3 million people.

French people are quite varied in appearance, reflecting the country's history as a crossroads of Europe. Early in its history, the region of France was already a melting pot of many tribes: Mediterranean, Alpine, and Nordic. The Celtic, Teutonic, Slavic, and Viking tribes brought with them different physical traits and customs.

Locals stopping for some ice cream in the town of Saint-Jean-de-Luz, Pyrénées.

From 1845 to the end of the 1960s, France had the largest population in Europe. In the 20th century France experienced a wave of immigration from Africa, Asia, and parts of southern Europe.

An extended family comes together to eat and catch up.

In the mid-19th century the need for workers brought an influx of immigrants from Belgium, Italy, and Poland. After World War I immigrants arrived from Algeria, Italy, Portugal, and Spain. Between 1956 and 1976 large numbers of Arabic and Jewish people left North Africa to settle in France.

Stereotypes abound. People expect the French from the north to be tall, blond, and blue-eyed. Northerners are sometimes perceived as more sophisticated than their southern neighbors, who are expected to be shorter, olive-skinned, dark-eyed, more easygoing, and slower-paced.

Such generalizations about the French quickly break down. The French are mobile within their borders, like many other populations. Large numbers have moved from village to city and from north to south in the pursuit of jobs and better lifestyles. In addition 10 percent of the French own second homes (a world record), often in regions far removed from their primary household, giving them roots in more than one region of the country.

Still the diverse French people appear somewhat homogeneous to outsiders. Perhaps what unifies them is the French language and the strong influence Paris exerts over the rest of the country. Most French people also share the unifying link of their unique history and culture, combined with a fierce love for their country.

Writer Christopher Sinclair-Stevenson in his book *When in France* observed: "The French are grumblers, but on one point they are united: France is, for all her faults, the best, most civilized, most beautiful country in the world."

CITY AND COUNTRY FOLK

France has at least 57 cities and towns with more than 100,000 people. The largest cities are Paris, Lyon, Marseille, Lille, Bordeaux, Toulouse, and Nice. During the postwar urbanization of France, Paris doubled in size, while the university town of Grenoble grew rapidly from 80,000 people to more than 405,000. About 80 percent of the population now lives in cities and towns, with the remaining 20 percent in rural areas.

About one-fifth of the total French population lives in greater metropolitan Paris. Paris is one of the world's most developed and densely populated cities. The first Parisians were a tribe of Gauls called the Parisii, who settled an island in the Seine River known as Île de la Cité. The majority of Parisians have moved out of Paris to live in the suburbs.

Today Paris is the capital of French government, business, and culture. It sets the trends for the rest of the country in fashion, intellectual life, and the arts. It is also one of the most beautiful cities in the world, with elegant restaurants and shops, famous museums and monuments, churches, plazas, boulevards, gardens and parks, and the picturesque Seine River. Paris is the home of many rich individuals, both French and foreign. Efficient but less attractive modern developments surround the city to house its expanding population.

Centers of population grew either to meet the demands of industry and trade or because of the amenities of resort areas, such as those along the Mediterranean Sea and in the warm, sunny towns in southern France. Most large cities are located near water: on the coast or along inland waterways.

Since the end of World War II, masses of villagers, especially young people, have moved to urban areas in search of better job opportunities and a more comfortable lifestyle. Some villages in poorer regions of the country are now almost deserted. The annual growth rate of urbanization is about 1 percent.

The beautiful Galeries Lafayette department store in Paris caters to the shopping needs of locals and tourists alike.

A recent countertrend has found young people moving back to the countryside to enjoy and protect France's natural environment, run small businesses, and produce crafts.

SOCIAL CLASSES

Although the feudal days of the monarchy and nobility are long past, social classes remain. The aristocracy maintains its inherited titles and property, and many members of the aristocracy live in elegant country chateaux and Parisian apartments. However, this class no longer dominates the country as it once did. Increasingly members of the old aristocracy have intermarried with wealthy members of the middle class.

A large number of French people belong to the petite bourgeoisie. They hold jobs in offices, such as in banks, and are, generally, quite well off. This allows them to pursue hobbies and luxuries that many may not be able to afford, including owning a light plane!

France has a large middle class, or *bourgeoisie*, that virtually runs the country. This class dominates the elite schools and universities. They are doctors, lawyers, teachers, bankers, and industrialists as well as sales executives, skilled technicians, newly rich merchants, and foreign-service professionals. Many leading politicians come from this class. The wealthier and more powerful members of the bourgeoisie make up about 15 percent of the labor force. A larger group (about 40 percent of the labor force), called the *petite bourgeoisie*, includes people in small- and medium-sized businesses, artists and intellectuals, and many office workers.

The working class includes farmers, makers of goods, and manual workers—about half of the labor force. This class may share lifestyle patterns with the middle class, but they do not advance through the state schools with the same degree of success. In spite of France's ideals of equality, less than 10 percent of university students come from the working class. A major gap between rich and poor still exists.

More conducive to the ideal of equality is the social welfare system. Rich and poor share equitably in such benefits as maternity care, bonuses for having children, day care for young children, general health and dental care, disability assistance, and retirement pensions. Around 17 percent of the

Regional variations in appearance and customs are most noticeable near the country's borders, where certain subgroups of the French population retain distinctive customs, languages, attitudes, and even styles of dress. For example, the people of Brittany, Bretons, express a strong individuality bearing the stamp of their Celtic origins. Regional pride has led many Bretons to retain their ancient language, folk festivals and traditional costume (right).

Also, the French of Alsace share favorite food, such as sauerkraut, with their German neighbors. Alsatians drink more beer than wine and speak a dialect mixed with German.

In southern France, many people in Provence have retained a Provençal dialect, influenced by their Roman heritage. These 100,000 Basques have a language unrelated to other European tongues and a unique heritage of folklore.

Like Bretons, the people of Corsica have a strong regional identity. Corsican separatists have begun to achieve their goals in seeking independence from France.

population is age 65 or older, which places a financial burden on workers to help support those who are retired.

France enjoys a low infant mortality rate, and the average life span is 78 years for men and 85 for women. In 2012 the population growth was 0.5 percent and the total fertility rate 2.08 children born per woman.

IMMIGRANTS' INFLUENCE ON FRENCH LIFE

Immigration has added to the diversity of the French population, at times raising questions about French identity and sparking social tensions. Many famous French citizens, from designer Pierre Cardin to actor Yves Montand, had foreign parents.

NON A L'EXCLUSION
FRANCE IMMIGRATION POUR TOUS LES SANS PAPIER
ABROGATION DES LOIS RACISTES XENOPHOBE!

Immigrant communities come together to demonstrate against racism in Paris.

Since the 1850s there has been a steady flow of immigrants into France. In 2008 approximately 19 percent of the French population was made up of immigrants. In the period between the world wars, France needed manpower and opened its doors to job-seekers, such as Italians and Poles, and refugees, such as Greeks, Armenians, Russians, and Spaniards. After World War II, immigrants (mainly young men) from Italy, Spain, Portugal, sub-Saharan Africa, the Middle East, and Asia arrived to aid France in its 30-year period of high economic growth. A rise in unemployment in the 1970s led to measures to curb immigration. There was a drop in immigration, and it consisted more of women and children reuniting with their families in France. About 800,000 French citizens returned from Algeria when it gained independence in 1962. Hundreds of thousands of immigrants have sought political refuge in France in recent years: Chileans, Iranians, Palestinians, Poles, and Vietnamese, and others from Latin America, Eastern Europe, and Russia. Most immigrants are legal; however, some come to France illegally.

Large groups of immigrants live in Paris and its environs and in the regions of the Rhône-Alps, Provence, and the Riviera. Large settlements of Muslims are concentrated in the port city of Marseille. The largest groups of immigrants in France are Algerians, Moroccans, and Polish.

France's ultra-right National Front Party, headed by Jean-Marie Le Pen, has responded to these new arrivals by encouraging racial intolerance. To counter that influence, a group of students formed SOS Racisme with the slogan *Ne touche pas à mon pote!* (neu TOOSH pah ah mohn POT), meaning "Don't touch my buddy!"

WHAT IS SO FRENCH ABOUT THE FRENCH?

The French exemplify strong individualism, value family life, and defend dearly what they consider their collective rights. They love life and the finer things in it, from food and wine to the arts. Many French people enjoy engaging in long and passionate conversations on any number of topics, in public or private settings. They share a conservative respect for tradition and a reverence for the past. French family ties are strong and most parents live close to their grown children, often taking an active role in raising their grandchildren.

The French take great pride in French products and French style. Many believe in preserving the purity of their beautiful language, going to great lengths to limit the import of foreign words into the daily vocabulary. The Academie Francaise is one such organization that polices the invasion of English words and phrases into the French language. Other French people believe that banning the use of English words is extreme and believe that languages should be allowed to change and modernize.

INTERNET LINKS

http://indexmundi.com/france/demographics_profile.html

This website provides detailed country statistics, charts, and maps compiled from multiple sources.

www.isj.org.uk/index.php4?id=565&issue=123

This website provides online articles from the journal *International Socialism* on the origins of the French working classes.

www.encyclopedia.com/topic/bourgeoisie.aspx

This website is an online dictionary and encyclopedia providing facts, information, and biographies on the middle classes, or bourgeoisie, in France.

LIFESTYLE

People shopping along the Rue de Caumartin in the IXe (9th) arrondissement of Paris.

7

THE FRENCH PEOPLE have varied customs and traditions. City life is not the same as country life, and different social classes behave differently. But *joie de vivre* (JWAH duh VE-vruh), a joy in living, is an essential element of every French lifestyle.

And *savoir faire* (SAH-vwahr FAIR), the ability to say and do the right thing in any situation, is one of the graces French parents hope to pass on to their children.

FAMILY TIES

The French cherish family ties. The family is a working unit, a community of interests, leisure pursuits, and affection.

Depending on income and social circumstances, different rates of child benefit, child care, and back-to-school allowances, housing and student accommodation grants, single-parent, and disability grants can be claimed by around 10 million French families. These claims are handled by the *Caisse d' Allocation Familiale* (CAF), or Family Allowance Office, which has about 20,000 employees.

In earlier times a large extended family of grandparents, parents, and children all lived together in one household. Today, as customs have changed and the birth rate is relatively low (around 12 births per 1,000 people), a typical family is smaller—just the parents and one to three children. Many children live at home and go to a school or a university near their home. When they marry French couples tend to settle not farther than about 10 miles (16 km) away from their childhood homes.

The French have a well-balanced lifestyle—they enjoy work and family life; they have an appreciation of fashion, the arts, good conversation, and delicious food and wine.

CITY LIFESTYLE

The pace of life in cities, especially in Paris, is faster and more frenzied than in the countryside. Traffic in the city center is more congested, and the sheer size of the population contributes to a hectic lifestyle. In the larger cities most people live in small apartments. The older buildings are often considered more attractive, with their handsome carved moldings and working fireplaces.

Zoning laws protect the environment of most French city centers, of which there are about 20, limiting building size and regulating traffic. Few buildings in French city centers rise higher than eight or nine floors. Rows of trees line the sides of main avenues, and flowers brighten the squares and central strips along main streets. Thousands of workers in green uniforms sweep the streets, keeping them clean.

In the cities, sidewalk cafés are one of the pivots of daily life. People linger, sipping a cup of coffee or a glass of wine, watching the world pass by. Café owners encourage patrons to stay as long as they wish. Famous writers Simone de Beauvoir and Jean-Paul Sartre wrote their books in a café on the Parisian Left Bank, the traditional heart of French intellectual, bohemian, and political life.

Cafés attract all manner of people, especially writers, artists, musicians, and students. Young people flirt and play jukeboxes and pinball machines in cafés. They also spend their free time in discos and shopping malls.

City streets are generally named after famous people, trades and professions, historical events, or artists. These names often change with changes in politics.

Paris is France's romantic capital city and receives tens of thousands of tourists annually. It is divided into 20 *arrondissements* (AH-rohn-DISS-mohn), or districts.

Surrounding the cities are burgeoning suburbs, often with massive government housing developments where poorer people can afford to live. More than half the urban population lives in new suburban houses or apartment buildings. Suburbanites commute to work on mass transit systems, such as the Métro in Paris, and other modes of public transportation.

The café is the meeting place for both the country and city folk. Here they spend long hours catching up on gossip or discussing politics and current affairs.

Some city dwellers feel that their housing is overcrowded and unhealthy. The richer suburbs are pleasant, but the poorer ones can be unattractive and rife with crime and racism. Those who can afford it escape to a second home in the country on weekends or vacations. Many have converted old farmhouses, deserted by previous owners who have moved to the city.

People in the cities tend to view country people as old-fashioned, stubbornly adhering to old habits, customs, values, and beliefs. On the other hand, they admire country people as the embodiment of hard work, individualism, frugality, and common sense. There is a growing nostalgia for the land and the way of life it represents.

The French, particularly young urbanites, are increasingly influenced by trends of modernization and "Americanization." They enjoy hamburgers, American movies, television programs, and popular music. Like young people the world over, many follow the American fashion of blue jeans, athletic shoes, and baseball jackets and caps.

RURAL LIFESTYLE

Many rural towns look almost the same as they did hundreds of years ago. In the heart of town is a square bordered by a church, small stores, and cafés. Old men play boules, or lawn bowling, while others chat and gossip. People sit in the cafés, eating and drinking, reading, writing, or playing chess.

Typical shops include the bakery, the butcher's, and the *charcuterie*, a type of delicatessen selling cooked meats and sausages. The *tabac* (tah-BAHK) sells stamps, newspapers, and cigarettes. Other small stores sell fresh fish, groceries, and various types of medicine.

Most rural people live in single-story dwellings. Their stone houses have brown, gray, or green wooden shutters. Villagers usually own a car, a television, and modern household appliances.

A typical village will have a belfry tower, a small post office, a café, one or two restaurants, a town hall with the French flag flying, and an elementary school. Many towns have a weekly outdoor market selling fresh produce, and sometimes, live chickens and rabbits.

Many people in the countryside are farmers or work in small businesses and have never traveled far from their villages.

EDUCATION

French schools are successful. An impressive 99 percent of the population aged 15 and above can read and write.

The French education system is based on discipline and innovation. Students are expected to work hard and participate actively in class.

Education is provided free by the government and is compulsory for children aged 6—16. The Ministry of National Education designs the curriculum and the examinations that students must pass. Children between the ages of 2 and 6 may attend nursery schools and kindergartens funded by the government. Reading is taught from age 5 onward.

Government, or public, schools are secular and do not teach religious education. Instead, civics is taught in accordance with the French Republic's core ideology of Liberty, Equality, and Fraternity. In 2004 a law was passed banning the wearing of religious symbols in schools and other public institutions. French families can choose to send their children to privately run religious schools. Most are Roman Catholic, but some are Protestant or Jewish schools. There are hardly any Muslim educational institutions in France. A law from 1959 allows private establishments to sign contracts to receive state funds in exchange for some state control. About 15 percent of French children attend private elementary schools and 23 percent attend private secondary schools.

French schools are highly competitive, expecting students to master a wide range of subjects. Discipline tends to be quite strict. Little time is devoted to afterschool activities or interschool sports competitions. French children have a very long school day (from 9:00 A.M. to 4:30 P.M., with an hour and a half for lunch) and usually two hours of daily homework. However, they can enjoy a long school vacation—about three months a year. Wednesday is usually a free day when schoolchildren can pursue games or cultural activities such as art, music, or dance, but many students must attend school on Saturday morning.

Secondary school consists of four years of *collège* (koh-LEHZH) and three years of *lycée* (lee-SAY), beginning at around age 11. After *collège*, some students continue their education at a vocational *lycée* to prepare for a job. Those with better grades fulfill the three years of general *lycée* to prepare for the baccalaureate exam, which they take when they are 18 or older. This exam is so difficult that roughly one-third of the students who take it fail.

The Sorbonne is one of the oldest universities in Paris, founded by the theologian Robert de Sorbon around 1257. Teaching at the university has become secular since the late 19th century. In May 1968 a protest initiated at the Sorbonne led to nationwide educational reform.

The Sorbonne has become one of the most famous institutions of higher learning in the world. It has outgrown its original home on the Left Bank and has expanded to 13 separate campuses.

Successful candidates for the baccalaureate receive free university education or attend one of the famous *grandes écoles*, elite colleges that train students for the top careers in government service, business, mathematics, and engineering.

The *grande école* L'Ecole Nationale d'Administration (ENA) has been called the most exclusive and prestigious school in France. Its students are almost certain that their intense study for two and a half years will lead them to the top in government or politics.

Military academies prepare students for military careers. Family tradition is strong here—eight out of ten students in these schools are children of active officers in the French armed forces.

ROLE OF WOMEN

Frenchwomen did not vote until 1945. Up to 1965 the husband was the legal head of the family, and the wife needed her husband's permission to get a job or a passport. The husband managed his wife's money and bank account.

French women today are achieving more equality. Birth control became available in 1967, and in 1975 abortion and divorce by mutual consent were legalized.

Today women are reaching prestigious positions in the business world. Although the law guarantees women equal pay, women's average salaries are still far below those of French men.

Women have long been influential in the French labor movement. As a group, they are taking an increasing interest in politics. They have been elected to parliament and to municipal councils. In 1991 Edith Cresson became the first woman prime minister of France. Other famous French women include Marie Antoinette (1795—92)—queen of France, who was executed during the French Revolution; Coco Chanel (1883—1971)—fashion designer; Marie Curie (1867—1934)—discoverer of radioactivity; Edith Piaf (1915—63)—singer and cabaret artist.

Many French people shake hands when meeting friends and acquaintances, even if it is for a brief moment on the street.

FRENCH CUSTOMS AND MANNERS

The French shake hands when greeting friends and saying good-bye. Close friends and relatives greet one another with a kiss on each cheek, and some southerners add a third kiss. Which cheek to kiss first varies depending on the region of France in which you live, so this custom can be confusing to visitors. French children expect to be greeted by being kissed. When a French person enters a room on a social occasion, the newcomer greets everyone in the room. Traditionally people call only close friends by their first names, although young people are often more informal about using first names. At work it is customary for colleagues to greet and say good-bye to each other with a handshake.

The French value politeness and rarely visit someone's home without an invitation. Invitations are usually answered in writing, and thank-you notes are sent soon after a party. Families enjoy sharing meals together. They gather around the table to feast together during holidays and important

THE FRENCH LOVE THEIR DOGS

The image of a well-dressed French woman dining in an elegant restaurant with a French poodle on her lap reflects the national passion for pet dogs. One French home in three has a dog. People walking in Paris reportedly step in dog droppings every 286th step! It is the city council that cleans up the mess, not the owners.

French thinker Blaise Pascal wrote in the 17th century: "The more I see of man, the more I love my dog." Dogs symbolizing faithfulness were carved on the tombs of French queens. Hunters, including French kings and noblemen, have long idolized their hounds. Napoleon had a favorite poodle named Moustache.

Along with pigs, French dogs, especially poodles, are used to sniff out the valuable underground truffles so highly prized in French cooking. (Unlike pigs, dogs can be trusted not to swallow the truffles.)

German shepherds, wirehaired dachshunds, Yorkshire terriers, and red cocker spaniels are among the most popular breeds with French pet owners. French dogs are often named for opera characters and figures in ancient history; common names include Rex, Fifi, Loulou, Princesse, and Whisky. The name Toutou is either supposed to sound like barking or stems from the word tu, *the familiar form of the word* you, *used to address children.*

On the outskirts of Paris, there is a private cemetery for dogs, the first in the world. Built at the end of the 19th century, it is the final resting place for the pets of both world-famous and unknown French dog lovers.

family events. Popular gifts to bring to a dinner party are a box of candy, cookies, a small plant, or an odd number of flowers, with the exception of the unlucky number 13. But a visitor should never bring chrysanthemums or white lilies, which are associated with funerals. French wine is also welcomed as gifts but is expected to be of the best quality. The French are fashion-conscious and dress smartly when invited out to dinner. It is important not to start eating before your host has wished all the guests "bon appétit." Some topics are not considered appropriate for polite conversation. The French do not like to discuss money matters or business during social meals.

Monsieur (meh-SYER) in French means "Mr." or "Sir"; *Madame* (mah-DAHM) means "Mrs.", "Madam", or "Ma'am"; and *Mademoiselle* (mahd-mwah-ZEHL) means "Miss" or "young lady." The term *Mademoiselle* has been banned from all official documents on the grounds that it is sexist. The French use these titles far more often than English-speaking people do, and they use them generally without adding the person's name: "*Bonjour* (bawn-ZHOOR), *Monsieur*" instead of "Hello, Mr. Jones." The second person singular *tu/toi* is reserved for close friends and family members of the same age or younger. The more formal second person form, *vous*, is used when speaking to superiors. However, the French are becoming less particular, and more and more people, regardless of age, are using the less formal *tu*.

The French have a love of debate, and enjoy expressing their true feelings with a gusto that might seem rude to people from other cultures. Conversations can become heated and the French like to use their hands to gesticulate when they are trying to put their views across in a discussion. Although gesticulating is acceptable, it is considered rude to point with one's index finger or to raise one's voice. The French can be critical of both government and business. Those who feel passionate about their cause sometimes get together for group protests, which occasionally grow into riots or strikes.

WORK AND TRAVEL

The typical working week in France is 35 hours. The French business day normally begins at around 9:00 A.M. and ends at 6:00 P.M. People work Monday to Friday and are expected to be prompt for appointments. Department stores are usually closed on Sunday and Monday. Most offices and shops close from noon to 2:00 P.M. Fathers and children used to come home for lunch, but with more mothers working, this practice is growing less common.

French workers are entitled to five weeks of vacation a year, and many divide this into three weeks of summer vacation in the month of August and two in the winter.

French cities generally have cheap and dependable bus service, and comfortable trains cross the country. The Paris subway system, the Métro, is one of the most efficient in the world. On buses and subways, people often give up their seats to senior citizens.

In cars children are required to ride in the back seat. By law every passenger in a car must wear a seat belt. It is illegal to honk the car horn in a town. Young people can ride motorized two-wheel mopeds from the age of 14.

INTERNET LINKS

www.justlanded.com/english/France/Articles/Culture/Social-customs-in-France

This website provides useful information about the main social customs of the French people, including types of greetings, appropriate topics of conversation, giving of gifts, dress code, and more.

www.frenchentree.com/fe-education/

This website provides information about a wide range of topics related to the French schooling system, including school selection, home schooling, and financial aid and going to university.

www.livingfrance.com/real-life-family-life-family-life-in-rural-france--49578

This website provides an interesting article on rural family life in France.

"It is hard to find a city-dweller in France who has not somewhere in the provinces a parcel of land to which he is strongly attached and to which, very often, it is his dream at last to retire. There is a peasant beneath the surface of every urban French-man. . ."— Waverley L. Root, 20th-century American journalist and food writer.

RELIGION

Notre Dame de Paris cathedral is one of the most enduring symbols of Paris.

F OR MUCH OF French history, religious differences have sparked conflicts and bloody wars. Most of the French are Roman Catholic. Roman Catholicism inspired the magnificent churches and cathedrals that are found in many parts of France.

In 1789 the state ceased to be officially Catholic. Napoleon's Concordat of 1801 recognized the Catholic Church as the religion of the majority and gave Protestants freedom of worship. In 1905 a law was passed clearly separating church and state. All citizens were guaranteed freedom of religious belief and practice. The French government is neutral in religious matters and tolerates the peaceful coexistence of different religious groups.

THE ROMAN CATHOLIC CHURCH TODAY

Between 83 and 88 percent of French people consider themselves Roman Catholic, and most have been baptized. Only about 21 percent, however, attend church regularly. Some sections of the country have a much higher percentage of practicing Catholics than others—up to 80 percent in those rural areas where religious traditions are strongest. Devout Catholics make pilgrimages to holy sites such as Lourdes, where the Virgin Mary is believed to have appeared in a vision.

People who rarely go to church may attend Mass during major events in their lives. Almost all Catholics are baptized, married, and buried by the Church. In France a religious ceremony does not constitute a legal marriage. After a christening, guests and children near the church receive blue or pink candy-coated almonds called *dragées* (drah-ZHAY). A special ceremony is held when children first receive Holy Communion and Confirmation at around age 11 or 12. They may be given a gift, wrapped in white. First Holy Communion is celebrated with a special lunch attended by the whole family. Only white food, such as chicken and white asparagus, is served.

The Roman Catholic Church has its own school system, newspapers, social service organizations, and youth groups. Critics of the French Roman Catholic Church claim that it is rigid, traditional, and distant.

The influence of the Church on the French people has diminished greatly. Fewer men now choose to become priests, and many people ignore Church doctrine forbidding divorce, abortion, and birth control. Further, many Catholic priests have been accused of pedophilia in recent times.

Recognizing a need for change, the Church has tried to reach out to more people, adapting to the needs of modern lifestyles without losing the traditions of the past. Prayer services were simplified in the 1960s, and Masses are now conducted in French rather than in Latin.

The Church has stepped up its involvement in progressive social action. Some worker-priests hold ordinary jobs and try to share the lives of the working class. An ecumenical outreach to non-Catholic Christians and to people of other religions marks the current attitude of the Catholic Church in France and the world.

Some conservative Church leaders, led by one of France's better-known and far-right former archbishops, Monseigneur Lefebvre, have reacted strongly against these liberalizing trends in the Church. About 10 percent of Catholics support a return to old-fashioned discipline and strict observance of doctrine.

PROTESTANTS IN FRANCE

Protestants, called Huguenots in France, were once spread throughout the country, but the 16th-century Wars of Religion and the revocation of the Edict of Nantes in 1685 greatly reduced their presence. Many children born to Protestant parents did not have civil status because Roman Catholic priests, the only ones authorized to conduct marriage services, refused to officiate at Protestant weddings. It was not until 1787 that the Promulgation of the Edict of Toleration partially restored the civil and religious rights of Protestants. Freedom of worship was eventually granted during the French Revolution.

A major French Protestant reformer was John Calvin (1509—64). He was educated in law and theology. *Institutes of the Christian Religion* was his

Devout Roman Catholics make pilgrimages to sites where they believe miracles have occurred. One much-visited shrine is in Lourdes in southwestern France. There, in 1858, Bernadette Soubirous, a sick 14-year-old girl from a poor family, said that the Virgin Mary had appeared to her. Altogether Bernadette had 18 visions. In the grotto where she said she had seen the Virgin, Bernadette had scratched the dry ground with her fingers and water had flowed out where no spring had existed before. The water appeared to have healing powers and, even a century and a half after, millions of people bathe in the water with hopes of being cured of their illnesses.

Church officials were initially skeptical, but decades later, after much inquiry, Rome declared the events at Lourdes miraculous. In 1933, 54 years after Bernadette's death at the age of 35, the Church canonized her as a saint. The world's largest underground church, capable of seating 20,000 to 30,000 people, was built to mark the 100th anniversary of the miracle. Around 5 million pilgrims visit Lourdes each year, with the largest of six yearly pilgrimages on August 15 (Assumption Day). People light candles and kneel to express their faith. They pray to the Virgin to cure their illnesses and disabilities. Discarded crutches are stacked at the entrance to the Cave of Apparitions.

The health of the local economy also benefits from the miracle. Lourdes has the largest number of hotel rooms of any French city except Paris. Souvenir shops sell plastic bottles in the shape of the Virgin, filled with holy water from the spring.

masterpiece, an important statement of Protestant belief. Calvin believed that human beings cannot save themselves from their sins, that only God can free them. He also believed in the Bible as the sole authority for the Christian faith.

Today about 2 percent of the French are Protestant, belonging to several different denominations. The leading one is the Reformed Church of France. Activities of all the Protestant churches are coordinated by the Protestant Federation of France. Protestants live in areas such as Paris, Alsace, the Jura Mountains, and the Massif Central. Although small in number, they are

INFLUENCE OF RELIGION ON FIRST NAMES

Since 1539 parents have been legally required to register their children's names. Until the Revolution, babies had to be named after a Roman Catholic saint. In addition to birthday celebrations, the French people sometimes also have a party on their Name Day, the feast day of the saint after whom they are named. Even non-Catholics tend to give their children the first names of Catholic saints. With certain exceptions, French citizens cannot legally change their names as registered at birth.

In 2004 a law was passed wherein French children are allowed to bear their mothers' surnames. Previously, parents had to pass on the name of a child's father, under a law that dated to 1794. Now parents may pass on the name of the father or the name of the mother, or both surnames in an order they may choose. The surname chosen for the first child of a couple must also be given to any other siblings.

Popular first names include Jean, Jacques, André, Claude, Michel, and Pierre for boys, and Marie, Jeanne, Françoise, Monique, Brigitte, Martine, and Sylvie for girls. Double first names, such as Jean-Pierre or Marie-Christine, are also a popular practice. Young modern parents are now picking names such as Lucas, Thomas, Hugo, and Théo for boys, and Camille, Manon, Chloé, and Léa for girls.

influential. They are active in French business and politics, with at least five appointed prime minister.

OTHER RELIGIONS

Between 5 and 10 percent of the French population are Muslims, making Islam the second-largest religion in France, after Roman Catholicism. The Muslim population includes many recent immigrants from North Africa. Muslims have settled mainly in Marseille and the immigrant neighborhoods of Paris.

There are more Jewish people living in France than in any other Western European country. About one percent of the French people are Jewish. They live in and around Paris, in Marseille, and in the larger towns in the eastern regions.

Anti-Semitic sentiments in the 7th and 14th centuries led to the expulsion of thousands of French Jews. Later they endured deportation to the death camps during World War II when France was occupied by Nazi Germany.

France imposed heavy penalties for racist, anti-Semitic, and xenophobic acts following attacks in the early 1990s by the extreme right-wing National Front Party and neo-Nazi groups on both the Muslim and Jewish communities and their mosques or synagogues, businesses, and cemeteries.

Jewish life thrives, marked by flourishing kosher restaurants, Hebrew schools, and synagogues. Still, Jewish children are usually given names of Catholic saints.

Small immigrant groups also practice Hinduism, Buddhism, and other religions. Newer groups, such as the Moonies and Hare Krishnas, have not gained a large following. Freemasons have a long history in France. They participate actively in politics, with a tendency toward leftist views. About 4 percent of the French declare themselves unaffiliated with any religion.

A French synagogue in Villeurbanne.

INTERNET LINKS

www.catholic-hierarchy.org/country/fr.html

This website provides comprehensive information about the Catholic churches in France, including current and former bishops, dioceses, events, and more.

www.state.gov/j/drl/rls/irf/2005/51552.htm

This is the official website of the U.S. Department of State, providing detailed information about France's International Religious Freedom Report 2005.

www.euro-islam.info/country-profiles/france/

This website provides news and analysis on Islam in Europe (including France) and North America, including information on demographics, education, organizations, and more.

LANGUAGE

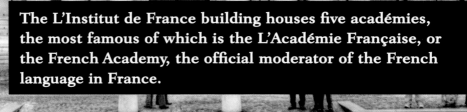

The L'Institut de France building houses five académies, the most famous of which is the L'Académie Française, or the French Academy, the official moderator of the French language in France.

O NE OF THE JEWELS of France is its official language, French. This precise and beautiful tongue has been a major factor unifying the diverse peoples of France and an ambassador for French culture around the world.

A LANGUAGE OF CLARITY AND BEAUTY

Many European intellectuals and leaders have preferred French to their native tongues. French has thrived as a language of diplomacy and, along with English, is one of the two working languages at the United Nations Secretariat.

French is the official language of 29 countries, including Canada, French Guyana, Haiti, Luxembourg, Monaco, and Switzerland. It is also used by French overseas *départements* and in many former French colonies. Between 70 million and 110 million people around the world speak French as their first language, and around 190 million more speak it as a second language.

The governments of French-speaking countries created an organization in 1970 called the Organisation Internationale de la Francophonie. It represents one of the biggest linguistic zones in the world. Its members share more than just a common language. They also share the humanist values promoted by the French language. The French language and its humanist values represent the two cornerstones on which the International Organisation of La Francophonie is based. Its members wrestle with world problems, agriculture, scientific research, and other areas of mutual concern. The University Agency

9

Like English, the French language is written using the 26 letters of the basic Latin script. Its unique features include the use of four diacritics, or accents, on vowels (ˆ), (´), (`), (¨), and the use of the cedilla (ç).

of Francophonie was founded in Montreal in 1961 to develop the exchanges and solidarity among universities teaching French.

SOURCES OF MODERN FRENCH

Along with Italian, Spanish, Portuguese, and others, French belongs to the family of Romance languages. These evolved from the Latin tongue used by the Roman conquerors. The people in the ancient region of modern France spoke a Celtic language known as Gaulish when the Romans conquered them. About 350 words in modern French can be traced to Gaulish.

The Frankish invasion contributed about 1,000 words to modern French, along with the name of the country. Danish Vikings added roughly 90 words. During the Renaissance many words came into the language from Latin and Greek. Neighbors Italy and Spain also contributed many words to French.

Women chatting on the streets of Paris. Regional dialects, some older than the French language, are still spoken in various parts of the country.

Old French was spoken from the 9th to the 14th century. It had two main Romance dialects: *langue d'oc* (or Occitan) in the south, and *langue d'oïl* in the north. *Oc* and *oïl* were the words, used to mean "yes." The northern Francien dialect became the standard French language of the country, because Paris was so influential. The dialect of the south survives in the regional dialect called Provençal.

In the 8th century, Emperor Charlemagne distinguished between the "rustic Romance tongue" and the "Latin tongue," and proposed that the former be used in church services. However, it was not until the 16th century that French totally replaced Latin as the language for official documents. The first known written document in French was the Oaths of Strasbourg, a treaty signed in A.D. 842.

Regional dialects are still spoken, especially at the edges of the country. They include Alsatian, Basque, Breton, Catalan, Flemish, and Provençal. As some dialects have diminished in importance, French scholars have grown increasingly interested in studying and preserving them.

THE ACADÉMIE FRANÇAISE

"It is a tradition solidly established in France to see in the purity of the language the image of the grandeur of the state."

—Linguist Claude Hagège

The official guardian of the purity and glory of French language and literature is the Académie Française, *or French Academy. Originally an informal coterie of literary men who met in Paris in the early 1630s to discuss rhetoric and criticism, the Academy was founded in 1635 by Cardinal de Richelieu. His goal was to make French a universal language, like Latin, and to make it clear and stable. He succeeded so well that the French language earned particular praise for the clear meaning of words and logical rules of grammar. These virtues are also assets in conducting international business and diplomacy.*

There are 40 Academy members, known as the 40 Immortals. They are chosen from among France's leading writers, scientists, politicians, military leaders, lawyers, and church leaders. The first woman member, Belgian-born author and U.S.-French citizen Marguerite Yourcenar, was elected in 1980; and the first Asian member, Chinese writer, poet, and translator François Cheng, was elected in 2002. Famous members include Victor Hugo, Voltaire, Alexandre Dumas, and Louis Pasteur. Members meet weekly, and they serve for life. They are initiated wearing ceremonial swords, cocked hats, and elaborate uniforms embroidered with green palms.

The Academy's main task is to write and edit The Dictionary of the French Academy (Le Dictionnaire de l'Académie française), *the ultimate authority on the French language. The Academy's work has discouraged rapid changes in the language, enabling modern readers to understand easily French literature written many centuries ago. Some have accused the Academy of being too conservative. However, after World War II, more than 2,000 English words entered the French language—words such as* le weekend, le drugstore, *and* le hamburger. *The awarding of literary prizes has also been an important function of the French Academy.*

The English language has been enriched by many French words and expressions, such as attaché, billet-doux, bon voyage, café, carte blanche, chalet, chef, civilisation, crème de la crème, de rigueur, fait accompli, faux pas, genre, glacial, réndez-vous, RSVP (répondez s'il vous plait), restaurant, valet, *and* vis-à-vis.

The English word billiards *comes from the French word* billard, employee *from* employé, employer *from* l'employeur, journalist *from* journaliste, merit *from* mériter, nonsense *from* non-sens, occasion *from* occasionner, platform *from* plateforme, rabble *from* râble, *and* telegraph *from* télégraphe.

KEEPING THE LANGUAGE PURE

The usage and pronunciation of French words are standardized throughout the country with the help of both the French educational system and the conservative French Academy. Thus, people from all parts of France and of every social class can easily understand one another.

In the 1970s the French government outlawed the use of any foreign word in official documents, on radio and television, and in advertising, if an equivalent French word already existed. Officially, the French view English words cropping up in their language as an invasion.

Unofficially, younger and more casual French people like the flexibility of English words and phrases. As writer Carl Bernstein observed that it is easy to combine words into catchy new expressions in English but almost impossible in French.

In matters of language, France has exported at least as much as it has imported. English has borrowed words from French since the Norman Conquest of England in 1066. It is estimated that 40 to 45 percent of all English words have French origins. Borrowed words reflect everything from religion—*pray*, *penance*, and *faith*—to French leadership in fashion and food—*chic*, *gourmet*, and *vogue*. French synonyms are generally more abstract and intellectual, and English synonyms more human and concrete. The French language has also lent countless words to languages in Europe, Asia, and Africa.

In 1991 the government decreed many radical spelling changes involving plural forms, hyphens (*le blue-jean* became *le bluejean*), and accent marks. The French Academy at first approved the changes, but later the members changed their minds and rejected the reforms. Many French writers organized to resist the changes, but there is a precedent for such rules imposed by language elitists.

French newspapers sold at a newsstand in Nice.

BODY LANGUAGE

You can tell whether people are French just by watching them talk. The French use their entire faces to emphasize what they are saying: raised eyebrows, wrinkled foreheads, broad smiles. Lips purse to form the vowel sounds. The hands are always moving, especially among people in the south.

French body language is fairly easy to understand. The shoulder shrug means "I don't know," "I don't care," or "There's nothing I can do about it." Two outstretched hands, palms up and fingers spread, can mean helplessness, anger, or indifference. A circle made of thumb and forefinger with the other three fingers raised means "okay" or, better yet, "perfect."

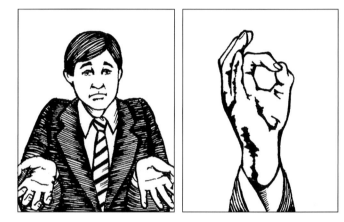

THE PRESS

Freedom of the French press is guaranteed by the Declaration of the Rights of Man. Since 1939 the number of daily newspapers published in France has shrunk from 220 to 86. National circulation stands at around 8.8 million readers.

In 2002 two free dailies, *Metro* and *20 Minutes*, began circulating in the public transportation systems in Paris, Lyon, and Marseille. These new papers strongly challenge leading ones like the liberal *Le Monde* (Luh Mohnd), or *The World*; the conservative *Le Figaro* (Luh Fee-gah-ROH); and the sports daily *L'Equipe* (L'ay-KEEP), or *The Team*.

Publishing has spread to the provinces. The avid French reader can pore over international, national, regional, and local news and get a wide range of political opinions. The regional paper with the widest circulation is *Ouest-France*, or *West-France*, published in Brittany's capital of Rennes. In total there are about 30 regional newspapers.

Magazine publishing has mushroomed in France, with the emergence of special-interest issues covering the youth market, sports, women's concerns, business, the media, religion, home improvement, health, the arts and sciences, and of course, the news. *Paris Match* is photojournalistic and is the most popular magazine in the news category. More popular still are the entertainment weeklies *Télé 7 Jours* (Tay-lay set ZHOOR), or *TV 7 Days*, and *Télé Z* (Tay-lay Zed), each with more than 1.8 million readers.

The L'Agence France-Presse (AFP) building in Paris.

Of the French-based international news agencies, the largest is L'Agence France-Presse (AFP), founded in 1944 and operating in about 165 countries around the world, of which 110 have AFP bureaus and about 50 are covered by local correspondents.

RADIO AND TELEVISION

The French government administers Radio France's seven stations, including France Culture, France Info, France Musique, as well as Radio France International's numerous stations, reaching an estimated potential audience of 80 million listeners worldwide. In addition, there are thousands of private, local radio stations broadcasting round-the-clock programs over AM and FM frequencies. Many stations now also broadcast over the Internet, so both radio and television broadcasts can reach a global audience.

Television was introduced in 1931, and France was one of the first countries to broadcast television programs. Almost every French home has at least one radio, 95 percent of French households have television, and owning a DVD player is equally widespread. There are six channels on the terrestrial network, one of them hosting the programs of the Franco-German joint venture the *Association Relative à la Télévision Européenne* (ARTE), plus many hundreds of different channels, general, regional, or thematic. The most viewed are private open channels TF1 and M6, and the pay-TV channel Canal Plus, with more than 6 million exclusive subscribers. The average person watches 23 hours of television per week in France.

Since 2005 France also offers *Télévision Numérique Terrestre* (TNT), or Terrestrial Numerical Television, to replace hertz frequencies with ground transmission. Today almost 95 percent of the population is expected to receive digital terrestrial television services. In 2008 five high-definition channels were launched— four free channels and one pay channel. About half of all programs shown on French television are imported from other countries, especially the United States. The government continues to uphold the educational and cultural level of French television and to resist American influences.

Many international magazines also include French editions to tap into the burgeoning magazine market in France.

INTERNET LINKS

www.frenchlanguageguide.com

This website provides guidance on various aspects of French, including vocabulary, grammar, and pronunciation as well as the history of the language.

www.academie-francaise.fr/

This is the official website of the Academie Francaise, providing information about the organization's role, its history, its members, and the dictionary.

www.nationmaster.com/country/fr-france/med-media

This Nation Master website provides detailed statistics and figures about the use of radio, television, newspapers, magazines, and other types of media in France.

ARTS

Juxtaposition of modern and classical architecture at the Musée du Louvre, one of the most famous museums in the world and a central landmark of Paris.

10

THE ARTS HAVE FLOURISHED IN France for thousands of years. Prehistoric drawings some 17,000 years old adorn the walls of the famous caves of Lascaux in southwestern France.

France is adorned with many styles of architecture, with ancient buildings often standing alongside controversial modern constructions.

THE GLORIES OF FRENCH ARCHITECTURE

Decorated prehistoric caves and Celtic graves containing jewelry and helmets are evidence of the earliest settlers. Roman civilization left marvels of construction—aqueducts, amphitheaters, and scattered ruins—throughout the country. In the Middle Ages, Romanesque churches, abbeys, and castles were built in a heavy and solid style, with round arches and flattened columns.

The Gothic style, from the mid-12th through the 15th centuries, made use of pointed arches, ribbed ceiling vaults, colorful stained-glass windows, delicate spires reaching to the heavens, and elaborate decoration with religious statues. Notre Dame Cathedral in Paris, built from 1163 to 1350, is famous for its daring, single-arched flying buttresses and its three 13th-century rose windows. The medieval abbey of Mont-Saint-Michel, off the coast of Normandy, has aspects of both Romanesque and Gothic styles.

Renaissance architecture from the 16th and 17th centuries revived classical forms such as the Roman arch, the dome, and Corinthian columns. Renaissance buildings, such as the *château* built for Francis I at Chambord, are harmonious and symmetrical.

Paris has become synonymous with mega-art exhibitions. In 2010, 26 million visitors (including foreigners) visited the many museums throughout France. From the Renaissance king François I to the Sun King, Louis XIV, and during the postwar years, France has prided itself on the massive state intervention that keeps its culture afloat.

THE EIFFEL TOWER

A symbol of Paris since it was built for France's Centennial Exposition of 1889, the striking 984-foot (300-m) Eiffel Tower was the tallest building in the world until 1930. Its construction of open-lattice wrought iron was a technological breakthrough, designed by bridge engineer Gustave Eiffel.

The revolutionary height and arresting design provoked great controversy 100 years ago. The tower was almost demolished in 1909 but was saved to house transmitters for the first transatlantic wireless telephones. Today the Eiffel Tower holds radio and television transmitters, three restaurants, a post office, and a steady stream of visitors who ride to the top for a dazzling view over Paris.

The Baroque period that followed saw an interest in the dramatic, luxurious, and sensual. Buildings combined architecture, painting, and sculpture and were integrated with elaborate gardens, lakes, fountains, clipped trees, hedges, and flowerbeds laid out in formal patterns, such as in the Tuileries and at Versailles. François Mansart's church of Val-de-Grâce in Paris is an excellent example of French Baroque—rich yet subtle.

Succeeding styles—Rococo (or Late Baroque), Neoclassical, Art Nouveau, Art Deco, Modern, and Postmodern—reflected the changing lifestyles of the French people and the new technologies available to builders. Emphasis shifted from buildings for the Church, kings, and nobles to structures for the public.

Baron Haussman's 19th-century urban plans enhanced Paris's beauty. Skyscrapers, where possible, were placed far from the center, with space reserved for parks. The Parisian sidewalks and wide, straight, tree-lined avenues were also his work. Different regions in France have their own distinctive architectural details, each town having its own unique charm.

CHATEAUX AND PALACES

Chateaux, combinations of the medieval feudal castle and the Italian villa, are among the most beautiful examples of French Renaissance and Gothic architecture. A string of beautiful chateaux stretches along the valley of the Loire River. Some of the finest are at Blois, Chambord, Amboise, Chaumont, and Chenonceaux. Most were built and redesigned over several centuries.

France's chateaux were often the stage of religious conflicts and quarrels over successions to the throne that sometimes led to murder and revenge. Many are still filled with elegant antique furnishings, paintings, and tapestries and are surrounded by gorgeous gardens. The château built for Francis I at Chambord has 440 rooms, 365 fireplaces, 13 great staircases, stables to hold 1,200 horses, and stands in a park surrounded by a wall 22 miles (35.4 km) in circumference.

The Château of Chenonceaux (below), which bridges the Cher River, was confiscated by François I. Later Henri II presented it to his favorite mistress, Diane de Poitiers. When Henri II died, his queen, Catherine de Médici, forced de Poitiers to exchange it for Chaumont-sur-Loire. The Château of Ussé looks like a fairy-tale castle and is said to have inspired the story of Sleeping Beauty.

Near Paris, the spectacular palaces of Versailles and Fontainebleau functioned as hunting lodges and homes for royalty and their retinue of thousands of nobles, servants, artists, and soldiers. At Fontainebleau, Louis XIV revoked the Edict of Nantes, France and Rome signed the Concordat, and Napoleon Bonaparte signed his abdication. The many important historical events that occurred at Versailles span the beginnings of the French Revolution to the signing, in its Hall of Mirrors, of the Treaty of Versailles by the Allies and Germany in 1919.

The Louvre museum in Paris has been under construction, on and off, since the 16th century and provides a unique showcase for the history of French architecture. In 1989 a new entrance was built—a 71-feet-high (22-m-high) steel and glass pyramid, designed by American architect I. M. Pei. The Louvre's painting collection is one of the largest in the world, representing all periods of European art up to the Impressionists.

VISUAL ARTS THAT ILLUMINATE OUR WORLD

The first paintings in France were the work of Cro-Magnon cave dwellers. They drew wild animals—reindeer, horses, and bison—on the walls of their caves, perhaps hoping for magical assistance in the hunt.

Manuscript illumination flourished in the Middle Ages, but a French school of painting emerged only in the 17th century. Leading baroque artists included Georges de La Tour and the Le Nain brothers. Claude Lorrain and Nicolas Poussin were masters of ideal landscape painting. Charles Le Brun was court painter to Louis XIV.

In the 18th century Rococo painters Jean-Antoine Watteau, François Boucher, and Jean-Honoré Fragonard were leading court artists who celebrated the theater and beauty and romance, while Jean-Baptiste-Siméon Chardin became known for simpler domestic scenes and still lifes. Elisabeth Vigée-Lebrun became popular as Marie Antoinette's portrait painter. Jacques-Louis David, court painter to Louis XVI, was the prime illustrator of the Revolution and the Napoleonic era. Romantic painter Eugène Delacroix's *The 28th July: Liberty Leading the People* was inspired by the French Revolution. Honoré Daumier satirized the professional classes. Also famous are the Classicist painter Jean-Baptiste-Camille Corot and Realists Jean-François Millet and Gustave Courbet.

Many important art movements began in Paris, even though many notable artists were of foreign birth, such as Marc Chagall, Salvador Dalí, Leonor Fini, Alberto Giacometti, Vincent Van Gogh, Amadeo Modigliani, Pablo Picasso, and Victor Vasarely.

Anyone who wishes to become familiar with French painting could do worse than to study the works of Edgar Degas, Edouard Manet, Pierre-Auguste Renoir, Claude Monet, Paul Gauguin, Henri Matisse, Henri Rousseau, Georges Braque, Paul Cézanne, or Henri de Toulouse-Lautrec. They have left vivid images of the people, landscape, food, and flowers of France.

Revolutionary art movements in France developed in stunning succession: Impressionism, Expressionism, Symbolism, Fauvism, Cubism, Dada, and Surrealism. Through their handling of line and color, painters expressed their personal emotions, dreams, and subconscious impulses or their cooler

French Impressionism is so widely loved today that it is hard to imagine the fury it provoked when its artists first showed their work in Paris. The appearance of Edouard Manet's Luncheon on the Grass *in an 1863 exhibition touched off the revolutionary new art movement.*

It was Claude Monet who gave the movement its name, from his 1872 An Impression, Sunrise *(right). The Impressionists organized eight of their own exhibitions in the 1870s and 1880s. The core artists were Monet, Sisley, Pissarro, and Renoir. Although their interests and styles differed, they cooperated in exhibiting their work and greatly influenced one another.*

The Impressionists stressed color and composition over story content, emotions, and symbols, and sought to capture the transient effects of light and color. They worked outdoors, used small canvases, and made freer brushstrokes to capture the quickly changing atmosphere. Collectors delight in the Impressionist images of light and color, sunny landscapes, and shimmering water.

Among the most fascinating Impressionist paintings are Monet's series of pictures of poplar trees, haystacks, water lilies, and the Rouen Cathedral. He painted the same scenes at different times of the day, trying to capture the fleeting effects of light on the ever-changing natural world. Renoir was known for sensuous, colorful pictures of pretty women and children and joyous crowd scenes. Degas portrayed bathers and dancers.

An assortment of styles and subjects characterized the many great Post-Impressionist artists who followed: Toulouse-Lautrec's Moulin Rouge cabaret dancers, Cézanne's landscapes

that so greatly influenced Cubism, Gauguin's exotic scenes of Tahiti and the South Pacific, and Dutch painter Van Gogh's colorful, often tortured still lifes and portraits. Van Gogh and Gauguin moved beyond Impressionism to use color for its emotional, expressive, and decorative elements.

After a long struggle for recognition, Impressionist and Post-Impressionist paintings received international critical approval and now sell for very high prices.

intellectual concerns. Twentieth-century local and foreign-born painters Balthus, Alberto Giacometti, Sonia Delaunay, Jean Dubuffet, Leonor Fini, Yves Klein, Victor Vasarely, and others turned out innovative masterpieces that have enriched museum collections around the world. But it is perhaps Matisse who is best remembered as one of the greatest French artists of the 20th century for his long, creative lifespan during which he produced a stunning array of works in varied styles.

French painters also applied their talents to sculpture, ceramics, collage, weaving and tapestry, and other decorative arts. Museums proudly display the sculptures of Degas, Dubuffet, Aristide Maillol, Jean Arp, Matisse, and many others. Probably France's foremost sculptor was Auguste Rodin (1840—1917), famous for the works *The Thinker* and *The Kiss*. Most major museums own copies of Rodin's work and there are museums in Paris, Philadelphia, and Tokyo dedicated to him.

The visual arts reach the public in many guises. American writer Richard Bernstein singled out the comic strip as the most popular cultural form in France. Called the *bande dessinée* (BAHND deh-see-NAY), or B. D. for short, this art form enjoys a large and devoted following. The Centre National de la Bande Dessinée et de l'Image (CNBDI) is France's national center for cartoons, comic strips, and illustration. Famous examples include *The Adventures of Tintin* and *Astérix*.

Made of bronze and marble, Auguste Rodin's *The Thinker* sculpture was first cast in 1902 and is now in the Musée Rodin in Paris. Often used to represent aspects of philosophy, this sculpture depicts a man in sober meditation while an internal struggle battles within.

LITERATURE OF IDEAS AND PASSION

French writers and thinkers have had a lasting impact on French politics, their ideas the seeds for riots, revolution, and reform. For example, philosopher Jean-Jacques Rousseau's *The Social Contract* is said to have inspired the French Revolution.

Of the poetry and love songs of medieval France, the best known are *The Romance of the Rose* and, earlier, *The Song of Roland*, a mid-11th-century epic based on a minor battle during Charlemagne's Spanish campaigns. France produced one of Europe's first professional woman writers, Christine de Pisan, born in 1364, who wrote numerous poems of courtly love, a biography of Charles V of France, and several works in defense of women. Marguerite de Navarre's remarkable *Heptameron*, published posthumously in 1558 and modeled on Boccaccio's *Decameron*, contained short stories told by fictional characters, probably one of the earliest French tales written in prose. One French work still popular today is *Gargantua and Pantagruel* by Renaissance writer and humanist François Rabelais, whose style of coarse humor gave rise to the term *Rabelaisian*. The Classical age was a high point in French literature, especially during the reign of Louis XIV. In the 17th and 18th centuries, playwrights Pierre Corneille and Jean Racine wrote tragedies, while Jean-Baptiste Poquelin Molière wrote comedies poking fun at human frailty.

French was the language of the educated class all over Europe, and French arts and literature were widely admired. The mathematician and creator of analytic geometry René Descartes wrote the famous words "I think, therefore I am," thus inspiring modern philosophy.

Eighteenth-century Enlightenment writers included the brilliant and prolific Voltaire. He opposed tyranny and prejudice and wrote lampoons on the French Regency and the famous satire *Candide*. Denis Diderot and Jean d'Alembert edited the *Encyclopédie*, an influential work of radical opinion. A Romantic reaction against the Age of Reason led to the glorification of emotion and imagination. Swiss-born Jean-Jacques Rousseau's *The Social Contract* argued that if a civil society could be based on a genuine social contract with individuals, men would obtain true political freedom. Poet, playwright, and novelist Victor Hugo was another leading Romantic writer. He wrote *The Hunchback of Notre-Dame* and *Les Misérables*, the latter heavily influenced by the Revolution and an appeal for social justice.

Alexandre Dumas's adventures *The Three Musketeers* and *The Count of Monte Cristo* are still enjoyed today. Jules Verne's novels were the forerunners of modern science fiction. An enduring favorite is Antoine de Saint-Exupéry's enchanting fable, *The Little Prince*.

George Sand (1804-76) was the most famous woman writer in 19th century France. She was a prolific and iconoclastic author of novels, stories, plays, essays, and memoirs; she represented the epitome of French Romantic idealism. Her first novel *Indiana*, the story of an unhappy wife who struggles

The title page of the first edition of *Les Misérables* by Victor Hugo.

"Man was born free, but he is everywhere in chains." — The opening lines of *The Social Contract.*

to free herself from the imprisonment of marriage (explicitly called a form of slavery). Her subsequent novels, such as *Valentine* and *Lélia* astounded readers with their frank exploration of women's sexual feelings and their passionate call for women's freedom to find emotional satisfaction.

Gustave Flaubert wrote his famous *Madame Bovary* in a realistic style. Émile Zola carried realism even further in a style called naturalism, exploring the squalid lives of the poor. The erudite man of letters, Anatole France, won the Nobel Prize for Literature in 1921.

In the early 1900s Marcel Proust wrote his epic *Remembrance of Things Past*, which many people consider the greatest modern French novel. André Gide won the Nobel Prize for literature in 1947 and raised ideas that led into the French Existentialism of the World War II period. Jean-Paul Sartre, Simone de Beauvoir, and Algerian-born Albert Camus developed these ideas of free will and moral responsibility in their novels and plays, and each won a Nobel Prize, although Sartre turned his down in 1964.

More recent writers of note include Alain Robbe-Grillet; Claude Simon, who won the Nobel Prize in 1985; Marguerite Duras; Nathalie Sarraute; Marguerite Yourcenar; and Michel Butor.

One of the best-loved French literary characters for children is Babar the Elephant, created by father and son Jean and Laurent de Brunhoff. One of France's more successful contemporary writers is Michel Houellebecq, whose book *Atomised* has received worldwide acclaim. Like many other French authors of today, Houellebecq writes about the crises facing his society, including the problems of immigration, racism, and the rise of American global cultural dominance. In 2011 a new literary award was launched called the "*Prix des prix littéraires*," which recognizes the work considered to be the "best of the best" from other existing main literary prizes.

FRENCH MUSIC

French music continues to delight audiences around the world. Georges Bizet's opera *Carmen* and Maurice Ravel's *Boléro* are well known from live performances and recordings, but also as background music to Olympic skating competitions and Hollywood films.

Until the 19th century France imported more music than it created. The few early French composers of note were François Couperin and Jean-Philippe Rameau in the 18th century. As with the other arts, the French appreciate originality and experimentation in music. Hector Berlioz and Claude Debussy were 19th-century pioneers whose influence in music mirrored the revolutionary contributions of French painters of their time. Debussy's subtle tonal shadings and the sense of painting a picture with sound have led critics to call it Impressionist. A leading 20th-century innovator, composer-conductor Pierre Boulez, created music in the 12-tone scale and also blended tape recordings with live music in a form called "concrete music." Olivier Messiaen introduced into Western music unfamiliar modes from the Middle Ages, music from Japan, rhythms from India, and sounds from nature, especially the songs of birds, and tried to express his Roman Catholic faith through music.

Municipal opera houses are found in many of the large cities, including the famous Paris Opera House. In Paris classical music is performed at the Conservatoire and the Salle des Concerts. Salle Pleyel is home to the Orchestre de Paris, and the Théâtre Musical de Paris houses the Orchestre National de France. Concerts are also regularly performed at the Théâtre des Champs-Elysées. Regional music festivals flourish, especially in the south. All forms of music, from chamber to jazz, have their stars and their enthusiastic fans.

After the United States, France is the world's second largest producer of hip-hop music. Most of its hip-hop and rap musicians come from impoverished urban backgrounds and grow up in and around France's major cities, including Paris, Marseilles, Lyon, and Toulouse. French rappers tend to be young and come from African and immigrant origins. The themes of their music are inspired by the social and political issues they face.

The opulent, 1,979-seat Palais Garnier opera house was completed in 1875 by architect Charles Garnier. The famous opera was used as the setting for Gaston Leroux's 1911 novel *The Phantom of the Opera.*

MINUET, CANCAN, AND BALLET

The minuet was a popular court dance from the 17th century for about 150 years, performed at first with small, graceful steps, then later with grand elegance. Ballet came to France from Italy and flourished from the 16th century. Its popularity waned but was revived in Paris around 1909 by the dazzling performances of the Ballets Russes, headed by Sergey Diaghilev. Popular 19th-century French ballets include *La Sylphide* and *Giselle*. French dancer and choreographer Marius Petipa created the immensely popular *Sleeping Beauty* and *The Nutcracker*.

Known for its high kicks revealing the petticoats and legs of the women dancers, the cancan became popular in Parisian dance halls in the 1830s. In the 19th century Jacques Offenbach created a French comic opera called the *opérette*, and his Gaîté Parisienne is still popular today. Today many ballet companies thrive in Paris and the provinces. Known internationally are the Lyon Opera Ballet and the prestigious Paris Opera Ballet School.

Dancers pose in front of the Moulin Rouge cabaret. The Moulin Rouge is best known for its French cancan shows and cabaret revues.

FILM

The French were major pioneers in filmmaking in the 1890s. The first motion picture was invented in 1895 by the French brothers Auguste and Louis Lumière. Some outstanding earlier directors were Marcel Pagnol, Marcel Carné, René Clair, Jean Renoir, and Jean Cocteau. Classic French films from the 1950s include the original *Cyrano de Bergerac* by José Ferrer, Roger Vadim's *And God Created Woman* (starring Brigitte Bardot), and Alain Resnais's *Hiroshima Mon Amour* (*Hiroshima My Love*).

Some important directors of the French New Wave (1958—64) were François Truffaut, Jean-Luc Godard, Claude Chabrol, Jacques Rivette, and Eric Rohmer. Focusing on film technique rather than plot, they often improvised their scripts. In the 1980s and 1990s, directors such as Luc Besson (*The Fifth Element*, *The Big Blue*) and Jean-Jacques Annaud (*The Name of the Rose*) turned to more elaborate sets and costumes. A landmark French film in 2001 was Jean-Pierre Jeunet's *Le fabuleux destín d'Amélie Poulain* (*Amélie*).

French films have been perceived by the rest of the world as sensual, poignant, political, literary, and highly personal visions of the human condition. The French produce about 150 full-length feature films each year. The annual international film festival at Cannes is the most prestigious in the industry. Producers represent a significant political lobby in France, which has enabled them to win, and defend, various helpful policies, including broadcasting quotas, which give them a strong bargaining position with television companies that need domestic films to strengthen their schedules. Co-producing with a French partner potentially opens up the wide array of state support systems. These support measures are a mixture of direct subsidies and levies. In 2011 a French film, *The Artist*, premiered at the Cannes Film Festival and proceeded to win many national and international accolades, demonstrating the vitality of the film industry. The film is unique because most of it is silent and produced in black and white.

INTERNET LINKS

www.culturecommunication.gouv.fr/

This is the official website of France's Ministry of Culture and Communication. The Ministry is responsible for managing the country's national museums and monuments and promoting and protecting the arts, including the national and regional archives.

www.louvre.fr/en/homepage

This is the official website of the Louvre museum, one of the largest and most-visited art museums in the world. The site includes information about its collection of more than 35,000 objects from prehistory to the 19th century.

www.alliancefr.org/

This official website of the French Alliance promotes the learning of the French language and cultural activities through its global cultural network in 136 countries.

LEISURE

Each September, hot-air balloonists from all over France come together for a competition in Rocamadour. Up to 25 balloons launch simultaneously from a small field in the bottom of a gorge in a spectacular show.

I N EARLIER TIMES the typical French farmer finished a long day of vigorous activity in the fields and spent any free hours quietly. Some favorite pastimes were discussing politics and relaxing by reading the paper or perhaps dozing under it.

Today many French people enjoy a shorter official work week of 35 hours, with five weeks of vacation. Most families enjoy gardening, working on home improvement, reading, and watching television. Increasingly they spend their leisure time plunging into active sports in the pursuit of physical fitness and "the good life."

More French schools are adding sports programs. Schools and communities are building more gyms, swimming pools, and playing fields. The sports-minded French have led in world-class sports competitions, winning many top honors in international competitions including the Olympic Games.

TEAM AND INDIVIDUAL SPORTS

The French play and watch soccer in huge numbers. Soccer clubs from every part of the country draw huge support—including famous teams such as Olympique de Marseille, Paris Saint-Germain, Olympique de Lyonnais. In 1998 the French national team, known as *Les Bleus* (the Blues) won the soccer World Cup for the first time. The same team won the European championships in 2000, meaning that for a two-year period, France was simultaneously world and European soccer champions. Basketball, volleyball, and rugby football (a style of football

11

• • • • • • • • • •

The French spend their leisure time entertaining themselves by the sea; in nature; in cities, towns, and villages; as well as enjoying historical, cultural, and sporting activities.

Hikers and climbers leaving for Mont Blanc, or "White Mountain," the highest of the peaks in the Graian Alps in Haute-Savoie.

named after Rugby School in the UK) are also very popular. In 2011 the French national rugby team reached the Rugby World Cup final, only to lose narrowly to New Zealand. In 2012 the French national rugby team was ranked third in the world. Both men and women compete in boxing, judo, and other individual contests.

The French can be quite serious about their sports, even wildly competitive. Cockfights in the north and bullfights in the south roused fierce passions in earlier times.

More popular than team sports are individual pursuits. The French ride horses and bicycles, jog, ice skate, camp, and hike. They climb mountains, and once up may choose to descend by hang gliding.

The French head to the water to swim, sail, canoe, windsurf, and water ski. They also ski over vast expanses of mountainous terrain. The 1992 Winter Olympic Games were hosted by Albertville in the Alps. In the Winter Olympics held in Vancouver in 2010, France won 11 medals. Fencing and cycling are their most successful sports. In the 2012 London Olympic Games, France won 34 metals.

Tennis is no longer a sport for the rich only, as each year more public courts are being built. Golf is still fairly exclusive, played on private courses in large cities and resort areas.

Spectator sports like horse races remain popular. Three famous auto races are the Le Mans 24-hour race, the Monte Carlo Rally, and the Grand Prix. Tennis championships, including the French Open (one of the international Grand Slam tournaments), and the Bol d'Or motorcycle race at Le Mans draw enthusiastic fans. The Tour de France, a 20-day bicycle race across the country, is France's most popular spectator sport.

TOUR DE FRANCE

Most daily activities all over France come to a halt during the annual Tour de France bicycle race. Millions watch it on television or go out to join the cheering crowds lining the 2,500-mile (4,022-km) route. Each July close to 200 professional racers from many countries compete in this event, although around 40 drop out before the end. Each racer must belong to a team of nine riders, with varying special skills in climbing or sprinting.

This race, held for the first time in 1903, winds through many regions of France, including extremely steep mountain roads. Those who finish ride proudly down the Champs-Elysées through the Arc de Triomphe in Paris. The cyclist with the best time at the end of each day wears the coveted yellow vest on the following day as he struggles to retain his lead.

The Tour de France means big business. Large sums are won and lost by gamblers on the race. The winning cyclist becomes a millionaire through endorsements and advertising, and manufacturers of cars, bicycles, sports clothes, and soft drinks compete to have their products appear on television being used by the heroes of the day. The Tour de France is open only to men. The shorter Tour de France Féminin was set up for women racers in 1984.

OTHER LEISURE PURSUITS

Guignol was a popular 18th-century puppet character. Today the name is used to refer to the puppet show.

French people pursue every kind of hobby, from photography to ceramics, from collecting antiques to playing musical instruments, from bird watching to stamp collecting. Like the farmers of old, the French still hunt and fish, and both freshwater and deep-sea fishing are popular leisure pursuits.

The French also read and watch television and attend cultural events in their leisure time. They enjoy Scrabble, crossword puzzles, card games, and chess.

It seems they follow Voltaire's advice to cultivate their gardens, and they spend significant amounts of time and money on improvements to their homes, including their vacation homes.

In the big cities, there is an abundance of things to do for leisure. Especially in Paris, families visit the many large and small museums, the aquarium, the planetarium, and the wax museum. Leisure in the parks is especially delightful for children, who enjoy puppet shows, donkey rides, sailing rented miniature boats on ponds, visiting zoos, and riding on carousels and miniature trains.

The French version of the Punch and Judy (British) puppet shows, known as *Théâtre Guignol* (teh-AH-truh guee-NYOHL), originated in the region of Lyonnais in the 19th century. Guignol, a hand puppet dressed in regional garb, with a short nose and round eyes, is always surprised and easily cheated but quick to get himself out of trouble and to help his friends. These shows demand active audience participation and teach the young audience about French culture and dialogue.

Parc Astérix, situated in the north of Paris, is a popular attraction and many families flock there every day. This theme park was inspired by the popular French cartoon strip about characters from ancient Gaul who resisted the Roman invasion of France 2,000 years ago.

Disneyland Paris in Marne-la-Vallée brings an international flavor to France's leisure scene. This $4.4 billion project covers more than 7.8 square

BOULES, PÉTANQUE, AND PELOTE

French men particularly enjoy boules, a form of bowling without the pins. Each player throws two large metal balls in turn at a smaller ball. The small target ball is called cochonnet *(koh-shuh-NAY), or piglet, and the object is to land your ball closest to it. The rules allow for knocking the other players' balls away, and onlookers are generous with advice to the players.*

Pétanque (peh-TAHNK) is a similar bowling game played with metal balls that are thrown into the air rather than rolled along the ground. It is particularly popular in the south, where groups gather in the village square for a casual game.

In the southwest people play the Basque game of pelote *(peh-LOHT). The players may wear gloves to hit the ball against a wall.*

miles (20.2 square km) of former sugar beet fields 20 miles (32 km) east of Paris. The whole park covers an area one-fifth the size of Paris. Both the Métro and the TGV bring visitors speedily to the theme park, where they can find accommodation in one of seven hotels. Although it features Mickey Mouse and all the other popular American attractions, Disneyland Paris has a more European flavor. For example, the new Discoveryland is based on the science fiction of French novelist Jules Verne, and Snow White speaks German.

The Disneyland Paris in Marne-la-Vallée is the second Disney resort to open outside the United States and the first to be owned and operated by Disney.

Frequent protests and demonstrations by farmers, former residents, and ultra-rightists have somewhat marred the success of Disneyland Paris, which experienced considerable losses during its first years of operation. Its opponents view it as an American product transplanted into the French countryside and thus a threat to their culture.

VACATIONS

In summer nearly half the French population heads for the beach, most often between July 14 and August 31, clogging the nation's highways. One-quarter of the French population vacations abroad, with Spain, Italy, and Greece among the more popular destinations.

A great interest in health also spills over into the choice of leisure activities. On the highways, rest stops have been set up to include running tracks, obstacle courses, and exercise equipment. Some vacation centers combine sports with such health treatments as seawater therapy and mud baths. Center Parcs, a popular vacation village near Paris, features a swimming pool with wave machines and water slides.

The French, like foreign tourists, sometimes take hot-air balloon rides through the wine country of the Loire Valley and Burgundy. They admire the countryside from barges that cruise the inland waterways. Other vacation activities include boating, painting, or retiring to a villa in the countryside.

Vacation resorts are also popular. In fact the ultimate leisure camp comes from France—Club Med, which operates about 80 resorts called "villages" around the world and attracts people from all over the world. Each Club Med destination offers equipment and lessons for a variety of sports, especially water sports. French tourists also enjoy sightseeing tours to historical sites in France and abroad, and others go on cultural vacations to learn a foreign language or improve their art skills.

Scouting camps have also become a popular leisure-time activity for young people under 18 years of age. There was no recognition for any Scouting training and qualifications until the 1990s. In 1998 the French government passed an act regulating camps and activities organized by recognized French Scouting Associations. However, this act was replaced in 2003 by new regulations, which do not include other member associations of the World Organization of the Scout Movement (WOSM).

The French enjoying a day at Lake Annecy in Haute-Savoie, a popular vacation destination known for its swimming and water sports. This lake is often described as "Europe's cleanest lake" because of environmental regulations imposed in the 1960s.

INTERNET LINKS

http://uk.franceguide.com/

This is the official website of the French Government Tourist Office that provides information on where to go and what to do in every region of the country.

www.letour.fr/le-tour/2013/us/

This official website of the famed Tour de France race includes information on the route, riders, teams, and coverage of past Tours.

http://en.france-montagnes.com/

This is the official website of the French ski resorts. It provides information on planning a mountain vacation, including activities, accommodation, holiday offers, resorts, and more.

www.kwintessential.co.uk/resources/global-etiquette/france-country-profile.html

The official website of France Culture provides updated information on the arts, literature, and the entertainment scene, including podcasts.

FESTIVALS

The carnival atmosphere of Mardi Gras is a very exciting time in France. Young people dress up in fancy costumes and enjoy parties throughout the night.

12

WHEN FRENCH CHILDREN GROW up and reminisce about their childhood, some of the happiest moments they recall are of celebrating festivals with their families. Some of these celebrations are widely known outside of France: Christmas, Easter, and New Year's festivities.

Others, such as the Bastille Day celebration, are uniquely French. In either case, the French observe these occasions with tremendous energy and style. And, naturally, every French celebration includes wonderful things to eat and drink.

PUBLIC HOLIDAYS

There are 11 public holidays in France representing religious, national, and historic reasons for celebration. When a public holiday falls on a Tuesday or Thursday, it is usual to take the Monday or Friday off as well, so that businesses may be closed for a long weekend—this practice is called "*faire le pont.*" On public holidays, some smaller supermarkets and bakeries may be open only in the morning.

Six religious holidays reflect France's Roman Catholic history: *Pâques* (PAH-kuh), or Easter (a Monday in March or April); Ascension Day (a Thursday in May); Pentecost (the 49th day or seventh Sunday after Easter); the Feast of the Assumption (August 15); *Toussaint* (too-SAN), or All Saints' Day (November 1); and *Noël* (noh-EL), or Christmas (December 25).

In France, some festivals are celebrated on a national level, while others are typical of the different regions, towns, and villages. Besides the major celebrations— Christmas, Bastille Day, and All Saints' Day—there are also music and food festivals galore.

Epiphany, celebrated on January 6, coinciding with Twelfth Night, 12 nights after Christmas is especially exciting for children. A large round pastry called la galette des rois *(lah gah-LEHT day RWAH), the cake of kings, containing a single bean (miniature porcelain statue), is served. The youngest child present cuts the cake and passes out the pieces. Whoever finds the bean becomes the king or queen for the holiday and chooses a royal mate.*

Candlemas, on February 2, is a religious holiday involving a Mass with candles carried in a procession. Families cook thin pancakes called crepes, and everyone tries flipping them. Legend has it that flipping the crepes while holding a coin will bring happiness and wealth.

Civil holidays include New Year's Day on January 1, Labor Day on May 1, and three additional dates that mark historical events.

Bastille Day, July 14, commemorates the storming of the Bastille prison in 1789, an event that sparked off the French Revolution. Also known as *Le Quatorze Juillet* (luh kah-TORZ zhwee-YAY), or July 14, this day is also France's national holiday. Tricolor flags appear on monuments and buses. Brass bands and military parades fill the streets. In Paris military troops parade past the French president, and people crowd around the monument to the Bastille, where there are bands and dances. After dark the skies blaze with fireworks, and crowds of people dance in the streets. A particularly spirited observance of this holiday in the medieval walled town of Carcassonne in the south is accompanied by spectacular fireworks and a festival of music, theater, and dance that lasts for two weeks.

Armistice Day, November 11, commemorates the end of World War I in 1918. Victory Day, May 8, celebrates the end of World War II in 1945. This holiday is sometimes called the Day of Liberty and Peace.

HOLIDAY REVELRY

Celebrations around Christmas and New Year's Day are particularly joyous. On Christmas Eve, French families gather to feast on turkey and, for dessert, a traditional Yule log, the *bûche de Noël* (byesh duh Noh-EL). Old and young share gifts, as in Christian countries around the world. Sometimes children put out their shoes at bedtime for *Père Noël* (PEHR Noh-EL), or Father Christmas, to fill with gifts during the night. Naughty children get a whip instead of toys, delivered by *Père Fouettard* (PEHR Foo-eh-TAHR), or Father Spanker. It was in the province of Alsace that Christmas trees first appeared in 1605. By the 19th century they had become popular all over Europe and in the United States. In the mountains at Christmas, skiers light up the night by descending the slopes with flaming torches.

New Year's Eve is celebrated with a feast and the honking of car horns at midnight. The following day people wish one another a Happy New Year and exchange gifts meant to bring good luck. Carnival, or Mardi Gras, is celebrated in many French cities on Shrove Tuesday, the last day before the Roman Catholic observance of Lent. The observance of Carnival in Nice, on the French Riviera, began sometime in the 13th century. Today partying goes on for weeks, with evening torchlight processions, parades of flower-covered floats, and huge groups of papier-mâché "big heads." Masked balls, confetti battles, flower tossing, and fireworks lead up to the moment when a model of King Carnival is set on fire, hanged, or drowned.

Crowds gather to watch the carnival parade from the grandstands in Place Masséna, in Nice.

April 1 is celebrated as *Poisson d'Avril* (pwah-SAWN dahv-REEL), or April Fish. This is something like April Fool's Day in the United States. In France people try to pin a paper fish on someone's back without being caught. They laugh and point to the victim calling, "*Poisson d'avril!*" The person who is fooled is supposed to give the pranksters a chocolate fish in return. Legend traces this holiday back to 1564, when Charles IX switched the beginning of the year from April 1 back to January 1. People protested mildly by exchanging silly gifts and playing pranks. Since the sun at the time was in Pisces (the zodiac sign featuring two fish), candy fish as well as paper fish became associated with the holiday.

In Brittany, men, women, and children wear charming traditional dress during local festivals.

On Easter Monday French children receive colored candy eggs and chocolate chickens. They may go to church in their best outfits and later hunt for Easter eggs. In France, handball playing is a traditional Easter amusement. The ball perhaps represents the sun, which is believed to take three leaps in rising on Easter morning. On Labor Day, which is celebrated on May 1, people exchange lilies of the valley and wear a blossom for good luck.

REGIONAL FESTIVALS AND SEASONAL EVENTS

Many areas of France have colorful festivals throughout the year. In Brittany, Quimper's Festival de Cornouaille, held every year since 1923, recalls the pre-Christian civilization of that region. Puppets act out Celtic tales, women demonstrate their embroidery skills, young girls model traditional lace headdresses, men engage in Breton wrestling matches, and people feast on grilled sardines and Breton crepes (KREH-puh) while listening to bagpipe music and watching clog-stomping dancers.

An unusual gathering takes place near the end of May in the Mediterranean village of Saintes-Maries-de-la-Mer in the Camargue. Thousands of Gypsies come from all over Europe to honor their patron saint—Sarah of Egypt. They hold a candlelight vigil, then march in a procession from the church of Saintes-Maries to the sea, carrying holy statues of Saint Mary Salome and Saint Mary Jacobe. There, the statues are immersed in water, and little paper boats, each containing a flickering flame, are released into the sea. As part of the festivities, famous Gypsy entertainers strum guitars and perform for the dancing and clapping crowd.

In a region already known for colorful bullfights, flamingos, and wild horses, the Gypsies add the dramatic finishing touch. Another pilgrimage in October also attracts many pilgrims and thousands of onlookers.

A traditional festival in Burgundy features a jousting contest on the Yonne River. Two men carrying poles and shields stand in longboats. As the boats are rowed toward one another at full speed, each contestant tries to push the other into the water. This jousting is said to show off the skills of loggers who used to ride logs floated downriver to Paris.

In Alsace a medieval festival at Ribeauvillé features knights in armor jousting, simulated bearbaiting, and parades of people grandly dressed as noble lords and ladies.

The Riviera city of Cannes welcomes up to 30,000 film professionals to perhaps the most important film festival of the calendar year. The judges at Cannes review films from many countries, and their awards are reported in newspapers all over the world. Glamorous people-watching is an added attraction at this two-week festival.

Les Trois Glorieuses (LAY TRWAH glaw-ree-YUHZ), the Three Glorious Days, in November is France's chief wine festival, one of many fall harvest festivals. Three cities in Burgundy share the honors, and all are world-famous in wine-tasting circles: Beaune, Clos-de-Vougeot, and Meursault. On Sunday a charity auction of wine is the highlight of the festival. On Monday professionals and amateurs alike indulge in spirited wine tasting and folk dancing.

Wine growers and drinkers also celebrate the appearance of the *Beaujolais Nouveau*, the new red wine in November. Grape harvest festivals, known as *Fête des Vendanges*, are widely celebrated in October. Members of old wine societies wear traditional clothes, and everyone tastes wine and dances. Even when it is not harvest time, the French can find a reason to rejoice. The wine villages pay tribute to their patron saint on Saint Vincent's Day, January 22.

In addition to the grapevine, harvest festivals honor other gifts of the land, such as peaches in Roussillon, lavender in Digne, and apple cider in Normandy.

The long summer vacations enjoyed by French children and their families also coincide with festivals in many southern cities. Elaborate programs of concerts and plays, folk dancing, parades, and feasting attract French and foreign tourists.

France has nearly 500 summer music festivals, ranging from concerts on boats and in churches and historic chateaux, to organ festivals in cathedrals with famous old organs, and festivals devoted to folk, chamber, or jazz music.

Paris celebrates summer with music, dance, and drama during the Festival of the Marais, a city neighborhood, from mid-June to mid-July. Later in the summer, during the *Festival Estival de Paris* (Paris Summer Festival), Parisians enjoy classical concerts in churches, museums, and concert halls. The *Festival d'Automne à Paris* continues Paris's arts celebrations through the fall months, with colorful dance, theater, and musical performances and art exhibitions.

Outside France, but within easy celebrating distance, are the festivals of Monaco, near Nice, such as the Monte-Carlo International Circus Festival in February, the Monte Carlo Motor Rally in January, the Monaco Grand Prix in May, and the International Fireworks Festival in midsummer.,

Many festivals in France celebrate major events in the Roman Catholic Church. Most villages honor their patron saint with a festival.

INTERNET LINKS

http://bastille-day.com/

This website provides information about Bastille Day, including its history and the biographies of important French revolutionaries.

www.festival-cannes.fr/

This is the official website of the Cannes Film Festival, with information about the forthcoming and past festivals plus archives.

www.discoverfrance.net/France/DF_holidays.shtml

This website provides a comprehensive listing of all the public holidays and special events celebrated in France.

FOOD

Different types of bread in a shop. Bread is eaten with most meals. There are many varieties of bread, but the crusty baguette (*bottom*) is the most common.

13

THE FRENCH people care passionately about food. They invest a significant amount of time and money in the pursuit of fine meals. The French insist on fresh ingredients of high quality and shop carefully for the best value.

Great care is given to the production of both raw and processed food. Each person involved in farming, marketing, and processing is an important and respected link in the food industry. Generations of families devote themselves to producing exquisite fruit, vegetables, and cheeses. They develop special breeds of chickens, ducks, geese, cows, sheep, and hogs to better satisfy demanding French homemakers and restaurant patrons.

The French have written extensively about food for centuries, so their cuisine is a rich field for study, with its own encyclopedias and histories full of original culinary genius and dynamic personalities. Rating restaurants is a national sport, and numerous guides on French food are published each year. The result is a cuisine with a wide-ranging influence on the food of other lands. International wine and food societies continue to celebrate the recipes of France's greatest chefs.

TYPES OF CUISINE

There are many types of meals to enjoy in France, depending on how much you can spend, where you are, and what you feel like eating. The most elaborate style of cooking, *haute cuisine* (OAT kwee-ZEEN), describes the grand meal of multiple courses served by top restaurants.

The famous *Michelin Guide* was first published in France in 1900 and today the guide awards one to three stars to a select number of outstanding restaurants throughout the world. In 2009 only 81 restaurants were given a rating by the *Guide*, with 26 of them being in France.

The hearty meals cooked at home for a family are known as *cuisine bourgeoise*, which overlaps with *cuisine régionale* (ray-zhuh-NAHL), or regional cooking—dishes made from locally available ingredients served in the provinces.

In certain restaurants, the chef offers a set menu with many courses of fairly small portions, giving a sampler of the chef's specialties and the best foods of the season and the region.

Nouvelle cuisine (noo-VELL kwee-ZEEN) refers to a recent trend among French chefs to serve lighter food with little or no butter, cream, or flour in the sauces. Food is arranged artistically on the plate, which may be decorated with edible flowers. Meat and vegetables are only lightly cooked. The low-calorie dishes of *cuisine minceur* (kwee-ZEEN man-SIR) were introduced in the 1970s by a French chef in an attempt to fuse dieting and weight control with fine French cooking.

REGIONAL FOODS AND DISHES

Different regions of France are famous for special foods and cooking styles unique to that area. Regional recipes are often passed down from one generation to the next, preserved on family stoves, in the kitchens of inns, and in restaurants from province to province.

The highly prized ingredients and distinctive styles of regional cuisines can also be sampled in Paris, which, like any other cosmopolitan city, offers a wide variety of food. However, the prices of regional dishes are much higher in Paris than in the provinces. The French appreciate good regional cooking in the provinces where the ducks are fattened, the fish caught, or the truffles unearthed. One of the most famous regional foods of France, pâté de foie gras (pah-TAY duh FWAH GRAH), the famous liver spread made from specially—and sometimes cruelly—fattened ducks or geese, comes from the Périgord region in southwestern France and also from Alsace.

There is food of almost unlimited variety and thousands of ways to prepare it throughout France. Some French foods use ingredients that may be unfamiliar to foreigners: sea urchins, eel, snails, kidneys, calf's head, pig's trotters, little birds such as woodcock and thrush, and all kinds of wild game.

The cassoulet is a French culinary classic. Experts say that a true cassoulet stew must consist of 30 percent pork sausage, mutton, or goose, with the remaining ingredients being white haricot beans, pork rinds, stock, and flavorings. The ingredients are pre-cooked separately in stages, then baked in layers in an earthenware pot known as a casserole.

In general, the cooking of northern France is based on butter, while southern French cooking uses olive oil, as does neighboring Italy. *Cuisine minceur* dishes use less butter and cream and more vegetable sauces.

The waters of the English Channel and the Atlantic Ocean yield many varieties of mussels, oysters, and fish. From Provence come olives and herbs—bay leaf, fennel, rosemary, and thyme. Excellent pork dishes (hams, pâtés, terrines, and sausages—known collectively as *charcuterie*) differ from one region of France to another.

A famous white or pink chewy candy called nougat, filled with chopped almonds and cherries comes from the town of Montélimar. Dijon exports several styles of mustard. Privas, near Lyon, produces *marrons glacés* (mah-ROHN glah-SAY), a delicacy of candied chestnuts. The region of Burgundy is known for snails, Cavaillon for melons, and Normandy for butter, cream, cheese, and sparkling cider.

French food lovers and foreign tourists travel to Mont-Saint-Michel in Normandy to sample the famous local omelets. They seek the finest *bouillabaisse* (boo-ya-BESS), a fragrant fish stew, in Marseille. They head west to Toulouse to sample the perfect *cassoulet* (kah-soo-LAY), a complex casserole of white beans, lamb, pork, sausage, and poultry.

The origin of many a recipe is revealed in its name: frog legs provençal from the province of Provence; salad niçoise, with olives, anchovies, tomatoes, and tuna, from the city of Nice; beef bourguignon, beef stew with onions and mushrooms simmered in red wine, from the province of Burgundy; quiche lorraine, a egg tart with bacon and cheese, from the province of Lorraine; calf's head à la lyonnaise, with chopped onions and parsley, as served in the city of Lyon; and veal à la normande, made with cream and Calvados apple brandy, from Normandy.

Provençal dishes often contain onions, garlic, tomatoes, and olives. An Alsatian dish, on the other hand, probably has sauerkraut somewhere in the recipe and is washed down with beer instead of wine. *Périgourdine* (pay-ree-gohr-DEEN) means there are luscious and expensive black truffles from Périgord in the sauce. French cheeses often bear the name of the town where

There are hundreds of different varieties of cheese to choose from in France. The most widely eaten is Camembert, a soft cheese made of cow's milk.

One of the most prized delicacies of French cuisine is the black truffle. This aromatic, black, warty fungus, which looks like a deformed avocado, grows underground in the roots of oak and hazelnut trees. Trained dogs and pigs are adept at sniffing out these hidden treasures. Because they have not yet been successfully cultivated by farmers,

truffles are rare. Scientists are trying to develop a machine to hunt them, claiming that pigs and dogs miss 80 percent of those in the ground.

Truffles are served whole or minced in sauces, eggs, and other dishes, providing a nutty flavor adored by the French. They are tastier fresh than canned, but are very expensive either way—a pound of the best truffles from the Périgord can easily cost thousands of dollars!

they are made, such as the world-famous blue-veined Roquefort made from ewe's milk and ripened in caves. France is known for Camembert, Brie, Port Salut (POR sah-LEWH), and more than 300 other kinds of cheeses, many of which are exported. The various cheeses made from goats' milk are called chèvres (SHEVR).

CAFÉS, BRASSERIES, BISTROS

There are many wonderful eateries in France. Cafés offer drinks and snacks and, in the larger cities, light meals. They may have outdoor seats along the sidewalk. Cafés are open long hours, sometimes around the clock, making them a popular spot to linger for gossip and perhaps a game of chess, dominoes, or table football.

The bistro (BEES-troh) ranges from the simple bar to the time-honored old restaurant with faithful patrons. Reflected in the decorated mirrors, waiters in blue aprons serve house specialties, omelets, steak with fries, and sometimes much fancier foods.

"The discovery of a new dish contributes more to the happiness of mankind than the discovery of a star." —Brillat-Savarin, author of *Physiologie du goût.*

The neighborhood café or bistro may be an endangered species, since so many are converting into fast-food places, fashionable restaurants, or North African kebab stalls.

A brasserie (BRASS-uh-REE) is a large, busy restaurant with waiters in white aprons. Traditionally a brasserie brewed beer; the cuisine is on the heavier side, with many Alsatian and seafood dishes. Tables are small and arranged in a cozy fashion.

An auberge (oh-BEHRZH) is an inn, usually in the country, serving drinks and complete meals. Occasionally they accommodate customers for the night.

Customary hours for most French restaurants are noon to 2:30 P.M. and 7:00 to 10:00 P.M., with later closings in Paris. Menus with prices are often freshly handwritten each day and are posted outside the restaurants.

A waiter looks over his diners at the busy Café de l'Olympia brasserie in Paris. The habit of sitting at a restaurant table for gossip and socializing is deeply ingrained in French society.

EATING THROUGHOUT THE DAY

In France families start the day with a small breakfast that usually consists of bread with butter and jam. They drink black coffee, coffee with hot milk, or the children's favorite—hot chocolate. Flaky, crescent-shaped rolls called croissants appear as a special treat.

The main meal of the day is often eaten at noon. It consists of several courses, beginning with an appetizer or soup. Steaks with French-fried potatoes or roast chicken served with vegetables are popular main courses. The salad, usually made of greens tossed with oil-and-vinegar dressing, follows as a separate course. A selection of cheeses may come next, and then fresh fruit or a pastry dessert to complete the meal.

People who do not go home for the midday meal may eat a lighter lunch of a quiche or sandwich in a restaurant. The evening meal, whether called dinner or supper, may be simpler than the large midday meal. A typical menu would be soup, a casserole, and bread and cheese.

A delectable array of French pastries is sold at this café in Paris.

Wine is usually served at lunch and dinner. Mineral water, plain or carbonated, may also be served. At festive meals, a different wine may be served with each course. Champagne is usually brought out for special occasions. After-dinner brandies or sweet drinks called liqueurs may be offered, along with strong black coffee served in small cups. The French add sugar but not cream to this coffee. At a very formal meal, a fish course comes between the appetizer and the meat.

Long, crisp loaves of French bread, called baguettes, accompany meals. Because this bread has no preservatives, the French buy it fresh each day. Brioche is a popular sweet, soft dinner bun.

Sunday dinners and grand occasions call for impressive desserts, such as the famed French pastries in a dazzling variety of shapes and flavors. Popular choices are fruit tarts, éclairs, and thin pancakes with sweet fillings. There are regional specialties and also desserts reserved for certain holidays and celebrations.

Like most Europeans, the French cut and eat food with the fork in their left hand and the knife in their right. They break off chunks of bread instead of slicing the baguette. Because the French love to talk, mealtimes are often very animated with interesting conversations.

WINES AND OTHER SPIRITS

France is famous for its excellent wines and bubbly champagnes. There are several important wine-producing regions, and each one makes a unique kind of wine. The shape of its bottle tells where a wine was made: Burgundy, Bordeaux, Alsace, Provence, or the Rhône Valley.

The year on a wine bottle is important, because changing weather conditions affect the flavor of the grapes. The prices also vary from year to year, with the greatest wines costing hundreds of dollars per bottle. Ordinary table wines are quite inexpensive.

Some wines improve with age and must rest in their bottles for years. Others can be drunk young. Many vineyards maintain huge wine cellars and offer tastings to the public in their tasting cellars.

Because French wines are so important to French prestige and the economy, the government inspects them to maintain their quality. Labels with the letters "AOC" indicate that a wine has been officially approved.

France also produces beer and cider. Aperitifs are appetizers drunk before meals. For example, the liquers Pernod and pastis have an anise flavor and are quite popular. After-dinner brandies, such as Armagnac and Cognac, are also commonly drunk.

Wine and other local produce displayed at a local shop. France produces approximately a quarter of the world's wines, and the French are the biggest drinkers of wine per capita in the world.

INTERNET LINKS

www.cuisine-france.com/

This website from Cuisine France provides a comprehensive list of traditional French dishes categorized by region or by dish.

www.foodbycountry.com/Algeria-to-France/France.html

This website outlines various aspects of French food, including information about its history and religious and celebratory foods, including popular recipes.

www.gourmetrecipe.com/recipes/type-of-cuisine/french-recipes

This website is dedicated to French regional products for the public, food professionals, and fine gourmets. It includes information about French gastronomy and the agro industry.

CLASSIC FRENCH OMELETTE

Makes 2 servings

3 medium eggs at room temperature

4 tablespoons (60 ml) unsalted butter

1 teaspoon (5 ml) finely, freshly grated Parmesan

2—3 chopped tarragon leaves

1 tablespoon (15 ml) each snipped chives and chopped chervil or parsley

Warm a non-stick frying pan on medium heat. Crack the eggs into a bowl and beat them with a fork so they break up and mix. With the heat on medium-hot, drop 2 tablespoons (30 ml) of butter into the pan. Season the eggs with the Parmesan, herbs, and a little salt and pepper, and pour into the pan. Let the eggs bubble for a couple of seconds, then take a wooden fork or spatula and gently draw the mixture in from the sides of the pan a few times, so it gathers in folds in the center. Leave for a few seconds, then stir again to lightly combine uncooked egg with cooked. Leave briefly again, and when partly cooked, stir a bit faster, stopping while there is some barely cooked egg left. With the pan flat on the heat, shake it back and forth a few times to settle the mixture. It should slide easily in the pan and look soft and moist on top. A quick burst of heat will brown the underside. Tilt the pan down away from you and let the omelette fall to the edge. Fold the side nearest to you over by a third with your fork, and keep it rolling over, so the omelette tips onto a plate—or fold it in half, if that's easier. Rub the other knob of butter over to glaze. Serve immediately.

CREPES

Makes 8 servings

2 cups (500 ml) all-purpose flour

1 cup (250 ml) milk

6 tablespoons (90 ml) butter, melted

3 medium eggs

4 tablespoons (60 ml) granulated sugar

Pinch of salt

Process the flour, butter, sugar, eggs and salt in a blender until the mixture is smooth. Add the milk ¼ cup at a time, until the batter is a liquid consistency. Set batter aside for 20 minutes. Melt a knob of butter in a crepe pan or large skillet over low-medium heat. Add 3 tablespoons (45 ml) of batter to the pan and swirl until the bottom of the pan is covered with batter. Cook the crepe for 1 minute, or until the crepe is slightly moist on top and golden underneath. Loosen the edges of the crepe, slide the spatula under it, and then gently flip it upside down into the pan. Cook for 1 minute and transfer the cooked crepe to a plate to keep warm. Serve with your choice of fruit, cream, or syrup.

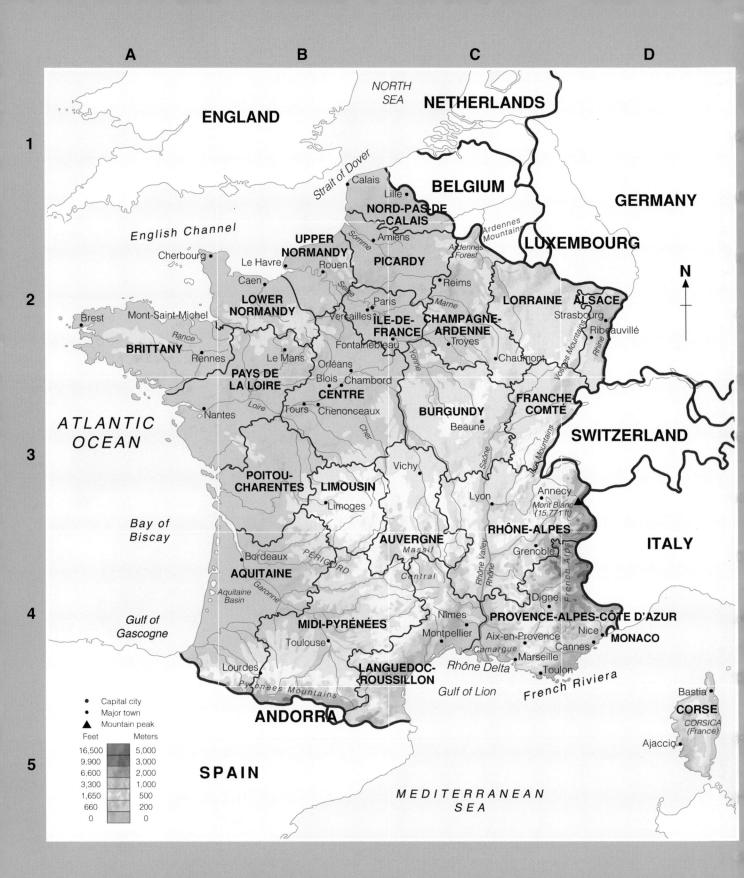

	A	B	C	D

1

ENGLAND

NORTH SEA

NETHERLANDS

GERMANY

Strait of Dover

Calais

Lille

BELGIUM

English Channel

Cherbourg

Le Havre

Rouen

NORD-PAS-DE-CALAIS

Somme

Amiens

Ardennes Mountains

Ardennes Forest

LUXEMBOURG

N

2

Caen

UPPER NORMANDY

PICARDY

Reims

Marne

LORRAINE

ALSACE

Brest

Mont-Saint-Michel

LOWER NORMANDY

Seine

Paris

Versailles

ÎLE-DE-FRANCE

CHAMPAGNE-ARDENNE

Troyes

Strasbourg

Ribeauvillé

Rance

Fontainebleau

Vosges Mountains

Rhine

BRITTANY

Rennes

Le Mans

Orléans

Chaumont

Yonne

3

ATLANTIC OCEAN

PAYS DE LA LOIRE

CENTRE

Loire

Nantes

Blois

Tours

Chambord

Chenonceaux

Cher

BURGUNDY

Beaune

FRANCHE-COMTÉ

Jura Mountains

SWITZERLAND

POITOU-CHARENTES

LIMOUSIN

Limoges

Vichy

Saône

Lyon

Annecy

Mont Blanc
(15,771 ft)

Bay of Biscay

AUVERGNE

Massif

RHÔNE-ALPES

Grenoble

ITALY

4

Bordeaux

PÉRIGORD

Central

Garonne

AQUITAINE

Aquitaine Basin

Rhône Valley

Rhône

French Alps

Gulf of Gascogne

MIDI-PYRÉNÉES

Nîmes

Montpellier

PROVENCE-ALPES-CÔTE D'AZUR

Digne

Nice

Cannes

MONACO

Toulouse

Aix-en-Provence

Camargue

Marseille

Toulon

Lourdes

LANGUEDOC-ROUSSILLON

Rhône Delta

French Riviera

Pyrénées Mountains

Gulf of Lion

Bastia

CORSE

*CORSICA
(France)*

5

● Capital city
● Major town
▲ Mountain peak

Feet	Meters
16,500	5,000
9,900	3,000
6,600	2,000
3,300	1,000
1,650	500
660	200
0	0

ANDORRA

SPAIN

MEDITERRANEAN SEA

Ajaccio

MAP OF FRANCE

ECONOMIC FRANCE

Services

✈ Airport

🚇 Eurotunnel

🚢 Port

🧑 Tourism

Manufacturing

✈ Aircraft

🧪 Chemicals

🧵 Textiles

🚗 Vehicles

Natural Resources

Al Aluminum

⚒ Iron and Steel

⚛ Nuclear Reactor

Farming

🐄 Dairy Products

🥬 Sugar Beet

🌾 Wheat

🍷 Wine and Spirits

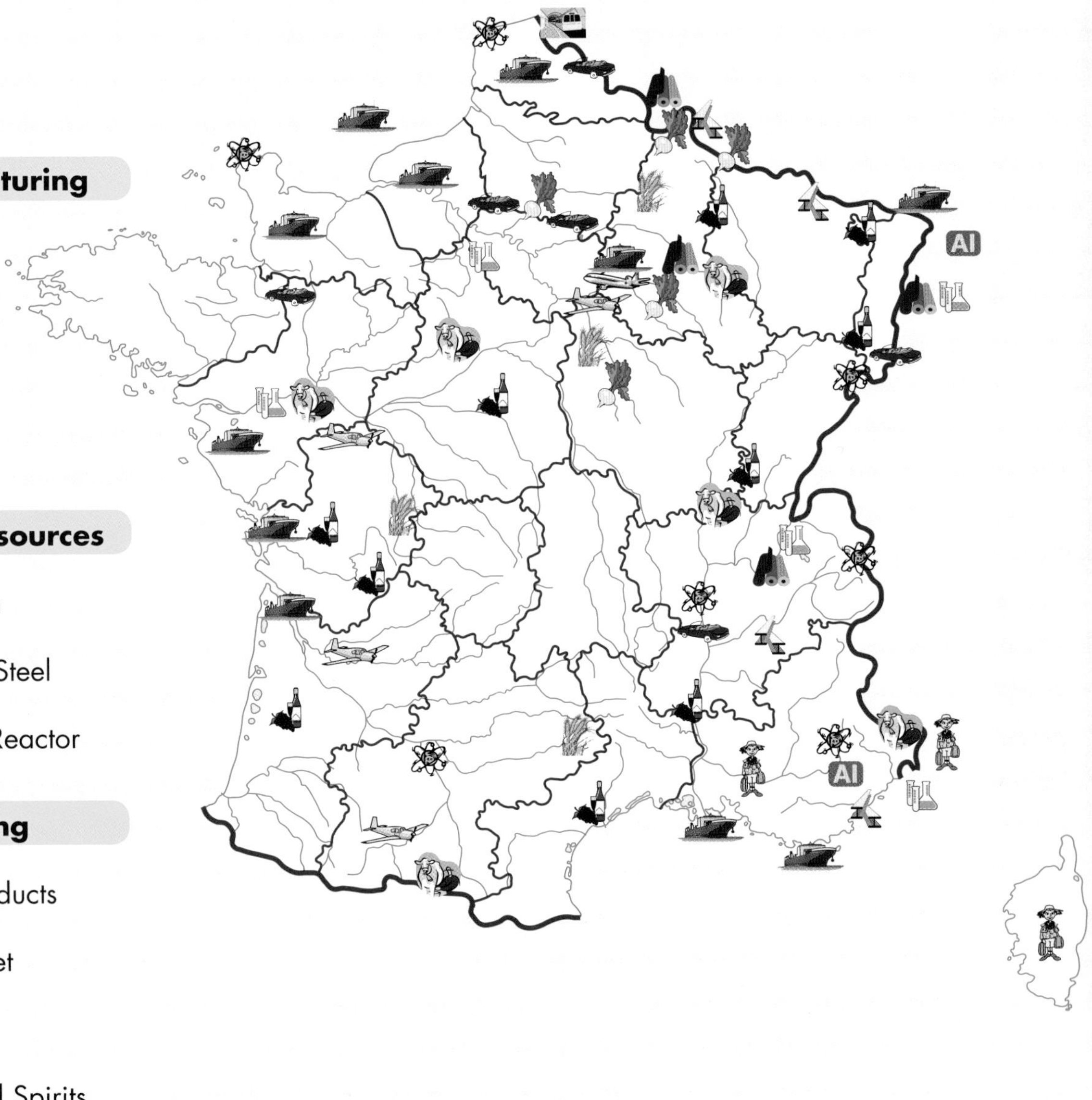

ABOUT THE ECONOMY

OVERVIEW

Like many parts of Europe, France is in the middle of a Eurozone crisis. Severe austerity measures are being implemented through cuts in government spending and tax credits in an attempt to control the budget deficit by 2013. The unemployment rate has been gradually rising from 7.4 percent in 2008 to 10.3 percent in 2012. The French economy has been embracing a more capitalistic model, moving away from public ownership. The telecommunications and banking sectors have been mostly privatized, including large corporations such as Air France and Renault. However, the government still maintains significant control in the power, public transportation, and defense sectors. France receives more than 75 million foreign visitors annually, and tourism is a major contributor to the economy.

GDP

US$2.253 trillion (2012 estimate)

CURRENCY

The euro (EUR) replaced the French franc (FRF) in 2002 at a fixed rate of 6.55957 French francs per euro.
1 euro (EUR) = 100 cents
US$1 = EUR 0.76 (April 2013 estimate)
Notes: 5, 10, 20, 50, 100, 200, 500 euro
Coins: 1, 2, 5, 10, 20, 50 cents; 1, 2 euro

GDP SECTORS

Agriculture 1.9 percent, industry 18.3 percent, services 79.8 percent (2012 estimate)

POPULATION

65,951,611 (2013 estimate)

LABOR FORCE

29.62 million (2013 estimate)

UNEMPLOYMENT

10.3 percent (2013 estimate)

MAJOR TRADE PARTNERS

Belgium, China, Germany, Italy, Netherlands, Spain, United Kingdom, United States

MAIN EXPORTS

Machinery and transportation equipment, aircraft, plastics, chemicals, pharmaceutical products, iron and steel, beverages

MAIN IMPORTS

Machinery and equipment, vehicles, crude oil, aircraft, plastics, chemicals

MAIN ENERGY SOURCE

Most (75 percent) of France's electricity comes from its 58 nuclear power plants. France is the world's largest nuclear power generator on a per capita basis.

COMMUNICATIONS MEDIA

Internet users: 45 million (2010 estimate)

PORTS AND HARBORS

Calais, Dunkerque, Le Havre, Marseille, Nantes, Paris, Rouen

CULTURAL FRANCE

Parc Astérix
Based on a famous comic character, Asterix the Gaul, this entertainment theme park 19 miles (30 km) north of Paris attracts families from all over the country when spring comes.

Mont-Saint-Michel
This is a circular rocky islet off the coast of Lower Normandy, north of Rennes. An oratory was built here in the eighth century by Saint Aubert, bishop of Avranches, after having a vision of the archangel Michael. The island was fortified in 1256 and resisted sieges during the Hundred Years' War and the French Wars of Religion. Napoleon used it as a state prison. In 1862 Mont-Saint-Michel was classified as a Historical Monument by the French and in 1979 UNESCO declared it a World Heritage Site.

Disneyland Resort Paris
This Disneyland theme park attracts about 12 million visitors every year. It is located east of Paris, just 35 minutes away by Métro.

Cathedral of Amiens
One of the biggest Romanesque and Gothic cathedrals in France, famous for its elaborate and creative features, such as its splendid rose windows and soaring nave. Building began in 1220 and was completed about 50 years later.

Eiffel Tower
Built for France's Centennial Exposition of 1889, it was never brought down and became Paris's favorite tourist landmark.

Notre Dame Cathedral
This impressive Gothic cathedral was built in Paris during the Middle Ages and modified through the centuries. It is best known as the home of the Hunchback of Notre Dame from a novel by Victor Hugo.

Louvre Museum
Formerly a palace for French kings, it is now a famous international museum in Paris, home to the mysterious *Mona Lisa*.

Palace of Versailles
The favorite castle of Louis XIV, the Sun King, built in the 17th century and famous for its gardens and water plays. The Treaty of Versailles was signed here, in the Hall of Mirrors, in1919 by the Allied and Associated Powers and by Germany. This palace still serves as a residence for visiting heads of state.

Arc de Triomphe
A famous Parisian monument celebrating Napoleon's military victories during the French Revolution.

24 Hours of Le Mans
Every year the biggest and longest auto race takes place here in the city of Le Mans. Lasting seven days, the 70th race was held in 2002.

Lascaux/Lascaux II caves
Discovered by some youths in 1940, its cave paintings of horses, stags, aurochs, ibex, and bison are famous. It is now closed to the public and reproductions of these paintings have been built next to the original cave.

Chateau of Chambord
This fairytale chateau is the largest of a string of ravishing Renaissance chateaux along the Loire River: Chenonceaux, Amboise, Blois, Cheverny, and Ussé. It was rebuilt by Francis I and Henry II, and Molière wrote here.

Lourdes
Some 6 million pilgrims visit Lourdes every year, where the Virgin Mary allegedly appeared in 1858. This site has a reputation for miracle healings.

Film Festival of Cannes
Started in 1946 and held every year in spring, this film festival in Cannes, near Nice, draws the crème de la crème of international actors and movie-makers.

ABOUT THE CULTURE

OFFICIAL NAME
French Republic

CAPITAL
Paris

NATIONAL FLAG
Adopted in the earlier days of the 1789 French Revolution, the tricolor French flag symbolizes royalty (white) and the capital, Paris (red and blue).

NATIONAL ANTHEM
La Marseillaise (Lah Mar-say-yez), or *The Song of Marseille*. A rousing tune composed by Claude-Joseph Rouget de Lisle in 1792, written to motivate revolution and inspire patriotism.

NATIONAL MOTTO
Liberté, Égalité, Fraternité (Liberty, Equality, Brotherhood)

ETHNIC GROUPS
Celtic and Latin majorities, with Teutonic, Slavic, North African, Indochinese, and Basque minorities

RELIGIOUS GROUPS
Roman Catholic, Muslim, Protestant, Jewish

LANGUAGES
French (official); main regional dialects: Alsatian, Basque, Breton, Catalan, Corsican, Flemish, Provençal

LIFE EXPECTANCY
85 years for women, 78 years for men (2012 estimate)

SYSTEM OF GOVERNMENT
Known as the Fifth Republic, a parliamentary democracy with a president elected by voters for a five-year term. The executive branch is the National Assembly, with 577 members elected for five-year terms by direct regional universal suffrage.

IMPORTANT ANNIVERSARIES
Labor Day (May 1), Victory Day (May 8), Bastille Day (July 14), Armistice Day (November 11)

LEADERS IN POLITICS
François Hollande—president (elected in 2012); Jean-Marc Ayrault—prime minister (appointed in May 2012).

OTHER FAMOUS PEOPLE
Victor Hugo (1802—85) Poet, novelist, and dramatist who wrote *Les Misérables* and *The Hunchback of Notre-Dame;*
Louis Pasteur (1822—95) Chemist and microbiologist; inventor of pasteurization;
Joan of Arc (1412—31) National heroine of France and a Roman Catholic saint;
Marie Curie (1867—1934) French-Polish physicist and chemist famous for her pioneering research on radioactivity.

TIMELINE

IN FRANCE	IN THE WORLD
17,000 B.C. Painting of the Lascaux caves	**753 B.C.** Rome is founded.
	116–17 B.C. The Roman Empire reaches its greatest extent, under Emperor Trajan (98–17).
58–51 B.C. Julius Caesar invades Gaul.	
A.D. 486 First Frankish kingdom established by Clovis.	**A.D. 600** Height of Mayan civilization.
771–814 Reign of Charlemagne, the greatest Carolingian ruler	
800 Opening of the first public schools	
987–996 Hugh Capet is named the first in a line of 13 Capetian kings.	**1000** The Chinese perfect gunpowder and begin to use it in warfare.
1163–1350 Construction of Notre-Dame Cathedral in Paris	
1337 Start of the Hundred Years' War with the English	
1430–31 Trial of Joan of Arc; she is burned at the stake in Rouen at the age of 19.	**1453** Turks take Constantinople, marking the end of the Byzantine Empire and the rise of the Ottoman Empire.
1643–1715 Reign of Louis XIV, the Sun King	**1776** U.S. Declaration of Independence.
1777 Marquis de Lafayette fights alongside George Washington for U.S. independence.	
1789 French Revolution begins.	
1793 King Louis XVI and Queen Marie Antoinette are guillotined. The First Republic is formed.	
1799 Napoleon becomes the emperor.	

IN FRANCE	IN THE WORLD
	1869 The Suez Canal is opened.
1870–71 War with Prussia. France loses Alsace and Lorraine.	
1889 The Eiffel Tower is erected.	
1918 The first Armistice Day. France recovers lost regions.	**1914** World War I begins.
	1933 Hitler rises to power in Germany.
1940 France surrenders to Germany.	**1939** World War II begins.
1944 D-Day (June 6). The Allied forces land on the shores of Normandy to liberate France.	**1945** The United States drops atomic bombs on Hiroshima and Nagasaki.
1969 Charles de Gaulle retires.	**1966–69** Chinese Cultural Revolution.
1981 François Mitterrand is elected president.	**1991** Break-up of the Soviet Union.
2002 Replacement of the French franc with the euro. Jacques Chirac is reelected president instead of right-wing extremist Jean-Marie Le Pen.	**2001** World population surpasses 6 billion. World Trade Center terrorist attacks in the United States.
2007 Nicolas Sarkozy is elected president heading a center-right government.	**2003** War in Iraq begins.
	2004 Eleven Asian countries are hit by giant tsunami, killing at least 225,000 people.
2008 France and other European governments pledge 1.8 trillion euros (US$2.3 trillion) to help stabilize the financial sector amid the global financial crisis.	**2008** Earthquake in Sichuan, China, kills 67,000.
	2009 Outbreak of flu virus H1N1 around the world.
2013 French military intervenes in Mali's civil war and recaptures Timbuktu from Islamic militants that invaded from northern Mali.	**2012** Hurricane Sandy devastated the northeastern United States.

GLOSSARY

aperitif
An alcoholic drink taken as an appetizer.

auberge
An inn, usually in the country, serving drinks, complete meals, and sometimes lodging.

bistro
An intimate, small, unpretentious, and inexpensive eatery, bar, or tavern.

bonjour (bawn-ZHOOR)
"Hello." An everyday greeting.

boules
A game of bowling without pins, popular in southern France.

brasserie
An informal restaurant serving simple, traditional fare.

brioche
A sweet, soft bun.

charcuterie
Cooked cold meats, usually pork (ham, sausages, pâtés), or a shop selling these.

château (SHAH-toe)
A castle, grand country home, or French vineyard estate.

crepe
A thin pancake, served with either sweet or savory toppings and/or stuffing.

cuisine minceur (kwee-ZEEN man-SIR)
Low-calorie dishes for the weight-conscious.

gendarme
State police officer serving in the armed forces.

grandes écoles (GRAHN-dzay-KOHL)
Elite colleges.

haute cuisine
Elaborate, high-quality cooking in the style of traditional French cuisine.

joie de vivre
Love of life, joy in living.

madame (mahd-DAHM)
Mrs., Madam.

mademoiselle (mahd-mwah-ZEHL)
Miss, young lady.

monsieur (meh-SYER)
Mr., Sir.

nouvelle cuisine
Dishes prepared and presented in a modern style with light sauces, using less butter, cream, and flour.

savoir faire
Ability to respond appropriately in any situation.

tabac (tah-BAHK)
Tobacco, or a shop selling newspapers, stamps, and cigarettes.

FOR FURTHER INFORMATION

BOOKS

Child, Julia. *My Life in France*. London: Duckworth, 2012.

Jenkins, Cecil. *A Brief History of France* (Brief Histories). London: Robinson, 2011.

Moireau, Fabrice. *Rooftops of Paris*. Singapore: Editions Didier Millet, 2010.

Moynahan, Brian. *The French Century: An Illustrated History of Modern France.* Paris: Flammarion, 2007.

Spenley, K., et al. *France*. London: Dorling Kindersley, 2011.

Steves, Rick and Smith, Steve. *Rick Steves's France 2012*. Berkeley, California: Avalon Travel Publishing, 2012.

Whittaker, Andrew. *Speak the Culture: France: Be Fluent in French Life and Culture.* London: Thorogood, 2007.

Williams, Nicola. *France: Country Guide* (Lonely Planet Country Guides). London: Lonely Planet Publications, 2011.

FILMS/DVDS

Stein, Rick. *Rick Stein's French Odyssey*. BBC Worldwide, 2007.

Steves, Rick. *Rick Steves's France. 2012*. Back Door Productions, 2011.

Voillet, Sandrine. *Paris—An Insider's Guide* (BBC). 2entertain, 2007.

MUSIC

Best of Edith Piaf, The. EMI Gold, 2008.

Canteloube, Joseph. *Songs of the Auvergne*. Alto, 2011.

Fleming, Renée. *Poémes*. Universal Music, 2012.

WEBSITES

French Agency for Environment and Energy Management. www.ademe.fr/anglais/vadefault.htm

French Ministry of Defense. www.defense.gouv.fr/

French Ministry of Foreign Affairs. www.diplomatie.gouv.fr/

French Ministry of the Environment. www.developpement-durable.gouv.fr/

French Senate. www.senat.fr/lng/en/index.html

Ministry for Social Affairs, Work, and Solidarity. www.travail.gouv.fr

Ministry of the Economy, Finance, and Industry. www.minefe.gouv.fr/ministere_finances/indexen.php

National Assembly. www.assemblee-nat.fr/english/index.asp

National Institute of Statistics and Economic Studies. www.insee.fr

BIBLIOGRAPHY

BOOKS

Bailey, Rosemary. *France*. New York: Dorling Kindersley, 2002.

Botting, Douglas. *Wild France: A Traveller's Guide* (Wild Guides). London: Sheldrake Press, 2000.

Doyle, William. *The Oxford History of the French Revolution*. New York: Oxford University Press, 2003.

Haine, Scott W. *The History of France*. Westport, CE: Greenwood, 2000.

Hargreaves, Alec. *Multi-Ethnic France: Immigration, Politics, Culture, and Society*. London: Routledge, 2007.

Ingham, Richard. *Nations of the World: France*. New York: Raintree Steck-Vaughan, 2000.

Mayle, Peter. *A Year in Provence*. New York: Alfred A. Knopf, 1990.

Mulvahill, Margaret. *The French Revolution*. New York: Franklin Watts, 1989.

Popkin, Jeremy D. *History of Modern France,* 2nd ed. London: Pearson Education, 2001.

Rothenberg, Gunther. *The Napoleonic Wars (Smithsonian History of Warfare)*. New York: Harper Perennial, 2006.

Smith, Timothy B. *France in Crisis: Welfare, Inequality, and Globalization since 1980*. Cambridge, UK: Cambridge University Press, 2004.

Steele, Ross. *The French Way: Aspects of Behavior, Attitudes, and Customs of French*. New York: McGraw-Hill, 2004.

WEBSITES

Ademe. www2.ademe.fr/servlet/KBaseShow?sort=-1&cid=96&m=3&catid=17571

Castelsagrat. http://property-castelsagrat.co.uk/how-many-french-people-own-a-second-home-or-holiday-home-in-france-where-are-their-holiday-homes-located.php

Central Intelligence Agency World Factbook (select "France" from the country list). www.cia.gov/cia/publications/factbook

Diplomatie. www.diplomatie.gouv.fr/en/spip.php?page=rubrique_imprim&id_rubrique=6925

Endangered Wildlife in France. www.kwintessential.co.uk/articles/france/Endangered-Wildlife-in-France/539

France environment. www.nationsencyclopedia.com/Europe/France-ENVIRONMENT.html

France-arts-revolution. www.guardian.co.uk/world/2011/mar/24/france-arts-revolution

Frenchentree. www.frenchentree.com/fe-education/DisplayArticle.asp?ID=95

Infomobil. http://infomobil.org/fr/content/newspapers-tv-and-radio

Nationmaster. www.nationmaster.com/red/country/fr-france/med-media&all=1

Parcs Nationaux de France. www.parcsnationaux-fr.com

Presidency of the French Republic. www.elysee.fr/

Prime Minister and Government of France. www.premier-ministre.gouv.fr/en

Pressreference. www.pressreference.com/Fa-Gu/France.html

U.S. Department of State. www.state.gov/r/pa/ei/bgn/3842.htm

INDEX

INDEX